HAROLD A. BRACK

Associate Professor of Speech and Homiletics
The Theological School, Drew University

Effective Oral Interpretation for Religious Leaders

PRENTICE-HALL, INC. ENGLEWOOD CLIFFS, N.J.

Library of Congress Catalog Card No.: 64-18621
PRINTED IN THE UNITED STATES OF AMERICA
[24427-C]

PRENTICE-HALL INTERNATIONAL, INC., *London*
PRENTICE-HALL OF AUSTRALIA, PTY., LTD., *Sydney*
PRENTICE-HALL OF CANADA, LTD., *Toronto*
PRENTICE-HALL OF INDIA (PRIVATE) LTD., *New Delhi*
PRENTICE-HALL OF JAPAN, INC., *Tokyo*
PRENTICE-HALL DE MEXICO, S.A., *Mexico City*

Preface

The need for religious leaders, ordained and lay, who can read aloud effectively and find satisfaction in doing so has prompted the writing of this book. Sections I (The Task of Oral Interpretation), II (The Act of Oral Interpretation), and III (Oral Interpretation of the Worship Service) will be equally useful to both laymen and clergymen. Section IV (Oral Interpretation of the Ritual) deals with services normally conducted by ordained persons only.

This book is intended for use by religious leaders who are already in the field, as a textbook to be used in schools where religious leaders are being trained, and as a resource for lay persons and lay groups. With the exception of two chapters (Chapter 12, Oral Interpretation of Prayers, and Chapter 15, Oral Interpretation of Hymns and Religious Poetry) no practice reading selections are provided. The reader may turn to a copy of the Bible or to the Hymnal or the ritual of his denomination, where he will find a wealth of material which may be read aloud.

No class assignments are provided. However, a teacher might use the last four chapters of Section III and the last four chapters of Section IV to provide a series of eight oral reading assignments. Each student would then read aloud before the class a prayer, a scripture lesson, a responsive reading, a hymn or religious poem, and a selection from each of the following services—baptism, communion, wedding, and funeral. In the case of the responsive reading, the class may serve as the congregation and read the responses. When making the assignments pertaining to the ritual, the instructor may wish to assign each person a different part of the ritual so that the class may hear the entire ritual read aloud and have the benefit of the instructor's comments on the various parts of the service.

In addition, I have found it helpful, in teaching this material, to utilize suggestions in Chapters 1 and 13 for additional class activities. Teachers specializing in the fields of Religious Music and Religious Literature have addressed the class. Another class session has been devoted to group dramatic reading of the Scriptures as discussed in Chapter 13. A bibliography is not appended, but the footnotes do suggest many valuable sources of additional information.

Lay persons who do not consider themselves leaders may also benefit from studying this book. Those who would like to gain a further appreciation of the Scriptures or religious verse through reading aloud and feeling their rhythm and mood will find this book helpful. Likewise, those who worship in a family or in some other small group where the leadership is rotated might find it possible to lift the level of the leadership of these groups by shared study of the suggestions found on the following pages.

The organization reflects the thesis that to improve his oral reading the reader needs an adequate understanding of oral reading and adequate skills of expression to perform the task. Hence, Section I deals with a study of the oral reading task and Section II with a discussion of the skills required for the act of oral interpretation. Sections III and IV deal with problems encountered in reading aloud the formal worship service and the ritual. Although many of the religious leader's tasks which require the use of oral reading are not discussed, the principles and skills presented herein will be valuable in the fulfillment of these tasks as well.

After more than a decade of teaching, I am sure that the great majority of religious leaders can improve their ability to read aloud, and increase the amount of satisfaction and pleasure they derive from doing so. It is my hope that their study of these pages will enable them to realize both of these goals.

May God bless to our understanding and use the principles and skills herein explained and described, and to His name be the praise and the glory.

Harold A. Brack

Contents

Part Two: THE ACT OF ORAL INTERPRETATION

Part Three: ORAL INTERPRETATION OF THE WORSHIP SERVICE

PART ONE: THE TASK OF ORAL INTERPRETATION

Chapter I

Reading Aloud and Leadership in Worship

. . . knowledge of God comes through people—people who can communicate. Communication is of the very essence of God. . . . As made in God's image, man's greatest gift is his ability to communicate.

BISHOP JAMES A. PIKE*

The ability to read aloud in a meaningful and moving manner is an important aid in our endeavor to lead people into genuine and satisfying worship experiences. Truly able reading of the ritual helps the members of the congregation fix their attention on the service. The elementary matter of fixing attention upon the words and acts of the service is frequently so difficult for the parishoner that, if the leader fails to command attention and guide it to the specific parts, the parishoner may spend his entire time in church without consciously participating in worship.

* *The New York Times,* April 2, 1961, Sec. 6, p. 39.

Moreover, good reading clarifies and emphasizes the crucial meanings of the words and acts of the worship service. Many worshipers are plagued by the crutches of habit and custom. They participate in the same acts, recite the same creeds, say the same prayers, and listen to familiar passages of Scripture with only faint and occasional contemplation of their meaning. An oral interpretation which sets forth the meaning of the service in a clear and emphatic manner disengages the worshiper from routine and engages him in a challenging experience, confronting him with the Word of God.

Effective oral reading will also arouse in the worshiper feelings of awe, wonder, love, and praise. Frequently the leader reads in such a restrained and disinterested way that the worshiper must surmount his manner and method in order to behold that which inspires these feelings. Many worship leaders read the service in a way that masks or conceals its true beauty and power.

In addition, a good oral interpretation will move at a pace that encourages and allows full participation and response by the attending congregation. If the congregation is given ample time to appreciate and respond to it at the proper places, the possibility of uniting the congregation in worship is greatly enhanced. The untrained or inexperienced reader rarely possesses the ability to give the congregation this sort of encouragement and opportunity; he hesitates to make effective use of pauses and shies away from changing the pace of his reading.

EXTENSIVE USE IN LEADING WORSHIP

The importance of striving to achieve the forementioned benefits of a good oral interpretation cannot be fully appreciated until one reflects on the meaning and significance of those portions of the ritual which are read aloud.

When we consider the units of the service which the leader reads aloud, the scripture lesson probably comes to mind first. This act alone would seem to be of sufficient magnitude to make every worship leader aspire to excellence in his ability to interpret orally, for Christians hold that the Scriptures contain all things necessary to salvation.

Surely a pastor should look with deep gratitude upon the opportunity to read the Bible regularly to his congregation in the context of the worship service. Here is a chance to share with his people his own love, reverence, and understanding of the Bible. Moreover, the context of the worship service does much to create a sense of expectation which assists the worshiper in giving his attention to the reading of the Word.

Teachers of literature frequently pause in a lecture to read aloud a portion of the work with which they are dealing. They know that an actual hearing will provide additional stimulation for appreciation and understanding of the work. "The late Oscar Hammerstein II, speaking of John Erskine, once recalled: 'I attended his classes in 1916, and one day John read a poem. It came to me with a shock that poetry was intended to mean something. Whatever I've done in the theatre I really owe to the way he read that poem.' "[1] Indeed, many believe that such things as rhythm, rhyme, and mood can only be comprehended and enjoyed through hearing the work read aloud. A regular opportunity to read aloud from the Scriptures should be an occasion cherished by every pastor.

The responsive reading in which the worshipers alternately share the reading of Scripture presents still another way of leading the congregation into a heightened awareness of its riches. Through the experience of the responsive reading, the pastor can encourage the members of the congregation to make a serious effort to interpret the Scriptures. Just as a musician discovers something new about a score as he plays it on his own instrument and a vocalist gains an additional appreciation for a libretto when he himself sings it, so the layman discovers new meaning and magnificence in God's Holy Word as he reads it aloud under the leadership of his pastor and in the company of his fellow Christians. As the pastor and the congregation help him enter fully into the act of expressing the insight and experience recorded in a particular passage, the worshiper rejoices in having found a new way of allowing God's Word to speak to him. No leader of worship should overlook the exciting teaching possibilities that are inherent in the shared oral reading of God's Word.

Equally gratifying for the worship leader is the opportunity to share with the congregation the beautiful, moving, and expressive prayers that are a part of the heritage and liturgy of his denomination. The opportunity to lead the congregation to the throne of grace—with the words of a prayer employed by Christians through the centuries as they have sought to commune with their God—is a rare and wondrous privilege.

---

[1] Clifton Fadiman, *Enter Conversing* (Cleveland, Ohio: The World Publishing Company, 1962), p. 299.

Every worship leader feels a responsibility for helping people to pray. He can fulfill this responsibility by leading the congregation in the use of prayers which have been treasured and preserved because they have assisted men in expressing their adoration and thanksgiving, in confessing their sins, and in dedicating themselves to God. Familiar examples are the prayers of General Confession and General Thanksgiving.

As the worship leader reads such prayers aloud, he can experience the joy of helping fellow worshipers pray—helping them say to God what they most need and want to say to Him. The chance to assist fellow worshipers to actually pray such meaningful and inspiring prayers ought to be keenly coveted by every worship leader.

In addition to those prayers which are offered jointly by the leader and the congregation, there are prayers which the pastor offers in behalf of the congregation, such as invocations, offertory prayers, and prayers of absolution. Such prayers, well read and devoutly offered, help the worshiper move closer to a genuine and satisfying communion with God. Ministers can sense this as they offer the Prayer of Absolution (forgiveness) in the communion ritual.

When the leader and the people join in a litany, the leader can give the congregation direct and repeated encouragement to enter fully into the act of prayer. The reciprocity of growing congregational response with intensified spiritual leadership can produce sublime moments of fellowship in prayer.

In some orders of worship the leader will also read "words of assurance" or "promises of pardon." These words should be read with great care and understanding. Their breadth and depth need full, total and effective interpretation. Their potential value to members of the congregation ought to be fully released through competent and persuasive interpretation. In a given worship service, prayer may well prove to be the most effective means of divine approach to the congregation.

The worship service is also enriched when the pastor reads with particular care the calls to participate in the various parts of the service, such as the call to worship, calls to prayer, and the call to present tithes and offerings.

If the pastor will read these directives in a way that makes the individual members of the congregation feel personally summoned to participate in the service, the people will be greatly aided in their endeavor to worship God "in spirit and in truth." Such verbal rubrics are the means by which the pastor may spiritually shepherd his people through the worship service. They ought to be read well.

In addition to the extensive use of oral reading in the regular worship service, we should observe that the major portion of the ministerial acts—weddings, funerals, baptism, holy communion, and reception of members—is read aloud. The personal, spiritual significance of these pastoral acts to the members of the congregation means that the pastor who earnestly strives for excellence in his oral interpretation will be rewarded with the experience of sharing their sacredness with his people.

As we contemplate the vast use which the religious leader is required to make of the art of oral interpretation, we might conclude that if he had to choose either speaking effectively or reading aloud effectively, he would be well advised to choose the skill of reading aloud. Where worship services are concerned, oral reading is not a secondary or auxiliary skill—it is a primary requirement for leadership which is adequate, helpful, and satisfying. Nothing less than a full and accurate communication of the Gospel is at stake.

CONTRIBUTION TO EXTEMPORANEOUS ASPECTS OF LEADERSHIP

Even if excellence in oral reading did no more than improve those parts of the worship service in which it was used, it would be a highly desirable skill. However, when we realize that it also improves the effectiveness of extemporary leadership, then its contribution becomes even more valuable.

For one thing, effective oral reading focuses the attention of the congregation on the Word which undergirds extemporary analysis and comment. If the congregation is moved to a thoughtful and careful hearing of the scripture lessons, there will be some background for the exegesis which is employed in the sermon. As Dean Charles Reynolds Brown observed, "Learn how to read your lessons aright and you will have taken a long stride toward giving your sermon a suitable setting." [2] Likewise, the portions of Scripture which were brought to the congregation's attention will provide a basis for some of the words of

---

[2] Charles Reynolds Brown, *The Art of Preaching* (New York: The Macmillan Company, 1922), pp. 205-6.

praise, thanksgiving, confession, and petition which are later used in the pastoral prayer.

Effective reading of scripture lessons not only draws attention to specific ideas and insights, but also stimulates the parishoner to give an appreciative hearing to the development and application of such ideas and insights. As we hear of a matter dealt with in the Scriptures, and as we are lead in prayer on this matter, we open our minds and hearts to what the worship leader may have to say about it in his extemporary message.

Indeed, reading these sections aloud helps the members of the congregation achieve a new orientation. They are able to listen and respond as children of God rather than as children of the world. This desire to hear and respond as a devout Christian is a favorable reaction to extemporary leadership. The spiritual climate created by these parts of the worship service which are read aloud can contribute a great deal to the effectiveness of extemporary leadership.

Another significant contribution of able oral interpretation is the improvement in the leader's choice of words and in his selection and arrangement of ideas. Improvements in style and content come about as the leader studies and practices those parts of the service which are read aloud. In order to read well, he has to ponder the words which are used and the manner in which they are employed. The ideas and insights they express are of even greater concern to the oral interpreter. Thorough familiarity with the liturgy and the Scriptures greatly assists the oral reader in selecting, arranging, and expressing his ideas in combinations of words which are accurate, understandable, forceful, and appropriate.

Beyond these fairly specific benefits, there is the development of an attitude toward the whole act of communication as it is involved in leading worship. The leader who senses that he is truly sharing an act of worship which is meaningful and spiritually helpful to the congregation will find it easier to pursue this goal during his extemporary leadership. This value of effective oral interpretation is emphasized by Norma Evans Koenig in her dissertation on "The Relation of Interpretative Reading to Preaching," in which she writes,

> Interpretative reading of literature *is* artistic delivery—the art of clearly and vividly expressing the whole meaning. Here is an area in which training is devoted to the very skill which the preacher seems to need . . . training in the principles of interpretative reading is valid either

> for preachers who read a complete manuscript just as the interpretative reader does, or for those who create as they go along, and preach from an outline . . . for modern teaching of interpretation . . . trains an attitude toward the whole speaking situation.[3]

Stevenson and Diehl go so far as to claim that every improvement in reading aloud will result in an improvement in public speaking:

> Every gain in effective public reading that we are able to consolidate will be a gain for more effective speaking. Learn the meaning of relaxation and breathing for public reading and you have learned it for speaking. Learn phrasing and emphasis, rate and range for reading and you increase your skills in these same variables for speaking.[4]

CONTRIBUTION TO THE INTENSITY AND TONE OF THE WORSHIP SERVICE

In addition to the inherent importance of each of the units read aloud and of their contribution to the extemporary portions of the service, we should also note their relation to the tone and intensity. In his Lyman Beecher Lectures, Sclater emphasized the importance of the principle of ascension in public worship. He speaks of a religious movement beginning with fear, ascending to awe, and finally to joy and love.[5]

Frequently the parts of the service which are read aloud merely continue on a plateau or even descend as the leader becomes fatigued or a bit indifferent. Often this is true because the leader has prepared by concentrating only on the parts, losing his vision of the whole. However, when even those few words which may be used to summon us to prayer, to confession, or to affirm our faith are read by an able reader, then we can sense the ascending nature of the worship service and participate in its progression.

In his work *Vocal and Literary Interpretation of the Bible,* Dr. Curry puts this matter before us in a forceful and succinct statement:

---

[3] Norma Evans Koenig, "The Relation of Interpretative Reading to Preaching" (Master of Arts Dissertation, University of Chicago, 1947), p. 5.

[4] Dwight E. Stevenson and Charles F. Diehl, *Reaching People from the Pulpit* (New York: Harper & Row, Publishers, 1958), p. 85.

[5] J. R. P. Sclater, *The Public Worship of God* (Garden City, New York: Doubleday & Company, Inc., 1927), p. 27.

> No matter what may be the form of worship there must be a struggle to lead the minds and hearts of men into an attitude of devotion. It is not a matter of words but of vocal expression. It is not a matter of mere intellectual domination but of spiritual leadership. Endeavoring to express the real feeling of the heart through the voice will enable a man to realize the possibility of bringing all parts of the service into a unity and giving intense progressive transitions from the lowest plane of the commonplace to the highest spiritual realization.[6]

IMPORTANT MEANS OF ENCOURAGING CHRISTIAN FELLOWSHIP

Skill in oral interpretation assists us in the immediate task of leading the service of worship. It also contributes to the achieving of some of the goals of worship. For example, it aids us in our effort to broaden and deepen the bonds of Christian fellowship. J. Edward Lantz maintains that the reader must share Biblical concepts and convictions with his hearers; he further urges the reader to concentrate on "sharing insights" with his hearers.[7]

It is in attempting to share our insights about the Bible and its concepts and convictions that we achieve a fellowship through God's Word. The shared struggle to comprehend God's Word to us constitutes a genuine spiritual fellowship. Moreover, our response to the Word of God may well lead us into shared experiences of praise, confession, and commitment.

In describing the fellowship of the early church, Harris Franklin Rall asserts that it was created by inner forces which were cohesive and life-giving. "Men came together by an inner compulsion; a common Lord, a common faith, devotion to a common task, the inspiration of a common hope, and a common spirit of goodwill united them." [8]

As we hear a meaningful and vital reading of Scripture and the liturgy, we have an opportunity to understand and appreciate anew those common inheritances of the faith which compel us to come together and which unite us in the bonds of Christian fellowship.

---

[6] S. S. Curry, *Vocal and Literary Interpretation of the Bible* (New York: The Macmillan Company, 1903), pp. 353-54.

[7] J. Edward Lantz, *Reading the Bible Aloud* (New York: The Macmillan Company, 1959), p. 45.

[8] Harris Franklin Rall, *Christianity, An Inquiry into Its Nature and Truth* (New York: Charles Scribner's Sons, 1947), p. 48.

STIMULUS TO BIBLICAL AND THEOLOGICAL INQUIRY

Biblical and theological inquiry is also stimulated by effective oral interpretation of the service of worship. When we are particularly moved by a passage of Scripture or a portion of the liturgy, we may be prompted to locate the selection and read it for ourselves. Satisfaction in our personal reading of the selection leads us to an examination of the context from which the selection comes.

As we receive insights and understanding from the Bible and the doctrine of the church, we are motivated to engage in a serious study of these sources. As we observe the benefits which fellow worshipers receive from the service of worship, we are prompted to make our own inquiry into the content and the meaning of the faith.

SUMMARY

As a religious leader, you need to become an effective oral interpreter. Worship services as well as the ministerial acts—administration of the sacraments, weddings, funerals—require extensive use of oral reading. Moreover, improvement in your ability to read aloud also contributes to your ability in extemporary leadership. In addition, you will improve the tone and intensity of worship services which you conduct, encourage Christian fellowship, and prompt Biblical and theological inquiry. As you study the following chapters keep in mind that (a) where the conducting of worship is concerned, skill in oral reading is a primary requirement and that (b) a full, accurate, and saving communication of the Gospel is at stake.

Chapter 2

The Relation of the Reader to His Material

His [the reader's] aim is to present the material so that it conveys the effect which the author intended. The writer is the creative artist; the interpreter, the re-creative artist.

CHARLOTTE I. LEE*

Oral interpreters have a variety of attitudes toward the material which they read aloud. Some choose to deal with their material at a deliberate distance so that they will not become unduly excited by it and thereby be moved to read at a rate or a degree of enthusiasm which might cause them to mispronounce words or to pause at awkward places. Others view the selection as demanding perfect pronunciation, pausing, and inflection; they move warily through the reading, anticipating that it will trip them up at any moment.

At the other extreme are those who seem to view the reading as a vehicle for manifesting their talents. They display their range, their ability to shout and whisper, their change of rate, and their skill in displaying a wide variety of feelings with little regard for the relation of these vocal efforts to the meaning of the selection.

Some view the selection as an assignment to be completed with dispatch—they read briskly with the intent of disposing of the material efficiently and in the allotted time. If meaning can also be com-

* *Oral Interpretation* (Boston: Houghton Mifflin Company, 1952), p. 12.

municated during this effort, well and good. However, the communication of meaning must not impair the efficiency or alter the time schedule.

The limitation of each of these attitudes can readily be seen. However, a more desirable relationship between the reader and his material may not be obvious. Therefore let us consider some relationships between a reader and the material to be read which bring about a more meaningful oral interpretation.

A STUDENT OF THE SELECTION

The reader may regard himself as a student of the selection. In this role he will inquire about the history of the selection. When was it written and in what historical context? How has the text been amended and why? In what way has it been used? By whom? How is it related to other pieces of literature? Elizabeth Janeway suggests the importance of the historical context when she observes that "All art is (among other things) a form of communication and identification. Literature is the way that a society talks to itself about itself." [1]

The oral interpreter will also consider the selection's form and style. At this point he will seek to distinguish it as prose or poetry. (He would also need to identify such things as drama, a letter, or an excerpt from a diary.) If it is prose, he will then strive to identify the type of prose —exposition, description, or narration. "The types of prose in the . . . Bible should be studied to understand the full implication of the literature. Wisdom literature, prophetic literature, and other less important types of prose are unique and the oral reader should know the general characteristics of each type." [2]

If the reader is going to interpret poetry, he will also want to determine the type of poetry. You will want to know if this is an Italian sonnet, an English ballad, or a piece of free verse. If your selection is none of the above but rather a piece of Hebrew poetry from the Old Testament, then you will want to be alert for various forms of parallelisms which the author used.

The reader will also be aided by considering the place which this

---

[1] *The New York Times,* August 13, 1961, Sec. 7, p. 1.

[2] Paul Hunsinger, "A Study of the Oral Interpretation of the King James Version of the Bible as the Scripture Lesson in the Sunday Worship Services of the Protestant Churches," *Summaries of Doctoral Dissertations,* Northwestern University, XIX (1951), 142-43.

selection holds in the field of literature. How a reader feels about a. selection, the joy he finds in reading it, and the eagerness with which he shares the selection with others all may be affected by his awareness of the literary stature of his selection. Surely the following paragraph by Bergan Evans would arouse one's appreciation for the King James Version of the Bible and prompt him to read passages from it with greater affection and respect.

> Written at the end of the Elizabethan age, when our language was in a ferment of magnificence, the King James Version of the Bible mingled grandeur and loveliness and joined beauty to splendor. It helped shape the English speaking peoples at the very time when they were shaping the world. For more than 200 years every literate person who spoke English was soaked in this book. His cradle was rocked to its cadences. All the dramatic moments of his existence borrowed dignity from its phrases. It inspired him in life and sustained him in death. Under the spell of its poetry, the preposterous was taken for granted and the incredible assumed to be axiomatic.[3]

Equally stimulating to his appreciation and expression would be the rhythm of Biblical prose, found especially in the Psalms, the book of Ruth, and Second Samuel. Such information about the literary value of your selection will enhance your impression of the selection as well as stimulate your expression of the ideas found therein.

A study of the selection's author should also be undertaken. The reader will be interested in the author's relation to his time and culture. Other works by this author may help the reader to understand this selection. The causes which the author supported, the political and religious views which he held, and the arts which he enjoyed all might assist the reader as he seeks to interpret the selection. In this regard, readings from the Old Testament will be strengthened by consulting a book like *Personalities of the Old Testament* by Fleming James.

The oral interpreter will do well to bear in mind Dr. Brigance's observation about words and the making of history. "Not only is history written with words. It is made with words. Literature in times of crisis becomes the words of men of action, of men who understand the power of words as weapons of warfare." [4] When interpreting the words of such men we will want to know of the action in which they are engaged

---

[3] Bergan Evans, "Thou Shalt Not or You Shall Not," *The New York Times Magazine,* March 26, 1961, p. 38.

[4] W. N. Brigance, ed., *History and Criticism of American Public Address* (New York: McGraw-Hill Book Company, Inc., 1943), p. vii.

and the warfare they are waging. If we were reading the words of Jeremiah, Professor Bewer's description of the prophet would help acquaint us with this background:

> The immediate occasion for the beginning of his prophetic activity was the Scythian invasion which threatened Palestine in 626. Anxiously the young man looked to the north; in a second vision it became plain to him that a fearful calamity would break in on his people from there, that Yahweh had summoned the northern armies to attack Jerusalem and the other Judean cities, because they had "forsaken Yahweh, burned incense to other gods and worshiped the work of their hands." Jeremiah must go and announce this to his people. He knew that it would not be easy, that it would bring him into sharp conflict with the leaders and the nation itself. But emboldened and empowered by Yahweh's own assurance of help, he spoke courageously his message in the face of persecution and death.[5]

As suggested earlier, the oral interpreter will want to give considerable thought to the meaning of a selection and the mood in which it was written. There are several possibilities for clues in the date or period of its composition. The date might be important in terms of the author's personal development. The degree of his emphasis or concern might be more clearly discernible if we knew in what period of his life the selection had been composed. The time might also be important in terms of the school of writing to which the author belonged. The positions taken and the endeavors engaged in by the group might reveal some important clues to the author's intent.

Then, of course, there is the location of the selection in history. The issues and forces of the day might well provide some telling insights into the author's meaning. If this material were written during Israel's exile or during a period of persecution of the early church, one might well expect that these conditions would have influenced the author.

The preceding suggestions are in accord with Geiger's "Dramatic Approach" to oral interpretation:

> We would suggest . . . that literature be approached by a study of its situation-attitude relationships. These terms respect the piece as a representation of experience, from which arguments may no doubt be drawn, but which is not itself an argument. To discover these relationships we ask ourselves who is doing what, how, where, when and why?

---

[5] Julius A. Bewer, *The Literature of the Old Testament* (New York: Columbia University Press, 1947), pp. 143-44.

> When we trace out the interactions of these elements we are tracing out what might be called the "logic" of the piece. But "logic" here is not something in contradistinction to "emotion"; it refers rather merely to the influences that elements of situation and attitude exert on one another. Since the influence of these elements is mutual we must consider the piece of literature as an organic unity. Situation and attitude are equally important in an organic relationship.[6]

The oral interpreter's first relationship to his material ought to be that of a student who seeks to know thoroughly and fully the selection which he is to interpret.

AN APPRECIATOR OF THE SELECTION

The second relationship to his material which will be helpful to the oral interpreter is that of an appreciator. If one is to read well, then he ought to provide himself with the leisure and the frame of mind which will allow him to focus on an appreciation of the selection. To put it another way, he should decide to treat himself to the luxury of appreciating literature.

Clarence T. Simon helps us envisage the scope of this relationship in his definition of appreciation.

> *Appreciation,* in the aesthetic sense, is something which the individual experiences in the presence of a work of art; a painting, a symphony, or a poem . . . it is the total reaction of the beholder to the work of art. . . . The meaning and significance of literature is grasped and its beauty sensed through action; the whole man does something. And it is this "doing something" that is appreciation.[7]

As this definition indicates, appreciation demands the full attention of the whole man. The fatigued, preoccupied, or distracted are not apt to experience any significant degree of appreciation. Usually appreciation cannot be hurried. Professor Clark warned, "Hurry, hurry, is the greatest enemy of literary appreciation and enjoyment."[8] Neither is

---

[6] Don Geiger, "A Dramatic Approach to Interpretative Analysis," *The Quarterly Journal of Speech,* XXXVIII, No. 2 (1952), 192.

[7] Clarence T. Simon, "Appreciation in Reading," *The Quarterly Journal of Speech,* XVI, No. 2 (1930), p. 190.

[8] S. H. Clark, *Interpretation of the Printed Page* (Chicago: Row Peterson & Co., 1915), p. 247.

appreciation likely to be nurtured when approached as a duty. If appreciation is viewed as something that is given to one by the work of art, it is more apt to be received by the reader than if he pictures himself as wresting an appreciation from the literary work.

Finally, it is important to note that although no adequate appreciation can be experienced without first studying the selection, careful study does not guarantee that one will automatically appreciate the selection. Appreciation is more than study.

In seeking to appreciate his selection, the reader might reflect on the deeper implications of its meaning. Or he might reacquaint himself with the style of the selection and explore its special features or merits. Another doorway to appreciation might be an effort to empathize with the author and the selection—to "feel one's way" into it. Holbrook Jackson describes this process for the reader of a novel: "He merges himself into the experience of the novelist, feeling, according to capacity, what the novelist felt when creating his characters and incidents, and weaving them in a consecutive, collateral narrative of his own." [9]

Let us sum up by saying that appreciation increases communicative effectiveness. It is the total reaction of the beholder to a work of art and it demands the full attention of the whole man. Appreciation goes beyond a study of the selection and may focus on meaning or style. Or one may seek to empathize with the author and the selection.

To conclude this plea for the reader to be an appreciator, let us ponder the words of British Author and teacher Lord David Cecil:

> Art is not like mathematics or philosophy. It is a subjective, sensual, and highly personal activity in which facts and ideas are the servants of fancy and feeling; and the artist's first aim is not truth but delight. Even when, like Spencer, he wishes to instruct, he seeks to do so by delighting. It follows that the primary object of a reader is to be delighted. His duty is to enjoy himself: His efforts should be directed to developing his faculty of appreciation.[10]

A SERVANT OF THE SELECTION

To communicate adequately the intellectual and emotional content of a selection, the reader must become its servant. He must give himself

[9] Holbrook Jackson, "Novelist and Reader," *The New York Times Book Review,* June 24, 1962, p. 2.

[10] Lord David Cecil, "The Art of Reading," *The Atlantic Monthly,* CLXXXV, No. 6 (1950), p. 73.

to the task of communicating the meaning in the mood or attitude which the author intended.

It is not the reader's task to alter or embellish the selection but rather to restrict himself to the content of the selection as it is actually expressed. His task is not to rewrite but to read what has been written.

Frequently readers need to be alerted to the necessity of making climactic that material which the author intended to be the climax. The preacher, for example, is inclined to emphasize a verse which he is taking for his text even though this verse is not the climactic verse in the Biblical passage.

The reader needs to understand that it is not he that is speaking, but the selection. The piece of literature is not simply a vehicle for his self-expression; he is the means by which this literature makes itself heard. Archbishop Whatley stresses this principle as it pertains to reading from the Bible:

> It is not, indeed, desirable that in reading the Bible, for example, or anything which is not intended to appear as his own composition, he should deliver what are, avowedly, another's sentiments in the same style, as if they were such as arose in his own mind; but it is desirable that he should deliver them as if he were reporting another's sentiments, which were both fully understood, and felt in all their force by the reporter. . . .[11]

As a servant, we must be willing to read vividly and with abandon. Oral reading of the selection must be the kind of reading which the selection merits, and not the kind in which we feel comfortable. We must be prepared to serve the selection adequately by constantly improving our skills in delivery.

Woolbert and Nelson, in their *Art of Interpretative Speech,* indicate the importance of being a servant of the selection in this manner when they write, "The ideal of the interpreter should be to do what the writer would do if he were a competent speaker and could meet face to face in conversation those who are to read what he writes." [12]

---

[11] Richard Whatley, *Elements of Rhetoric* (Boston: James Monroe and Company, 1844), pp. 270-71.

[12] C. H. Woolbert and S. E. Nelson, *The Art of Interpretative Speech* (New York: F. S. Crofts & Co., 1929), p. 19.

A SHARER OF THE SELECTION

". . . the whole thing is bound up in wanting to communicate something you like to others and have them like it, too." In those words Charles Laughton underscored the fourth relationship to the material which is being read: namely, it is something to be shared and you are the one to share it.[13]

This is to say that the oral interpreter cares about how he is being heard as well as what is being heard. His goal is that the listener shall appreciate this selection even as he appreciates it. His aim is more than attentiveness, understanding, or admiration. He wants his hearers to share his affection for the selection. It is the pleasure which the oral interpreter covets for his hearers and which he strives to share with them. As sharers of a piece of literature we do not dispense it, but rather we lead our listeners into a more perceptive beholding of it. "The reader faces in both directions at once, toward the literature as the source of his inner gestures and toward the audience whose imagination these gestures can reach out to and capture. . . . He apparently communicates the story or poem out to us, but actually he leads us to a communion in it."[14]

Everyone who attempts to read aloud should avoid being deterred by a lesser goal. Many readers never get beyond the aim of an accurate or correct reading. It is only when we become a sharer of the selection that we get beyond communicating the "letter" and begin to communicate the "spirit."

George Santayana, in an essay entitled "The Idler and His Works," gives a self-appraisal of his work and attempts to evaluate it from the standpoint of posterity. Santayana's concluding sentences are very suggestive for the oral interpreter: "Therefore the truest picture of my inmost being would show none of the features of my person, and nothing of the background of my life. It would show only the light of understanding that burned within me and, as far as it could, consumed and purified all the rest."[15] It is something very much like this that the

---

[13] Charles Laughton, "Storytelling," *The Atlantic Monthly,* CLXXXV, No. 6 (1950), p. 72.

[14] David W. Thompson, "Interpretative Reading As Symbolic Action," *Quarterly Journal of Speech,* XLII, No. 4 (1956), p. 394.

[15] George Santayana, "The Idler and His Works," *The Saturday Review,* May 15, 1954, p. 50.

oral interpreter wants to eventuate out of his relationship with the literature he is to read aloud. He wants the light of his understanding to consume and purify his background and the features of his person so that it is communicated through his oral interpretation.

As we strive to become sharers of our selections, let us be encouraged by Charles Laughton's observation about reading aloud: "The communion that happens . . . is one of the best things we have in life." [16]

SUMMARY

Readers may feel quite differently toward the same selection. Let five ministers undertake the reading of Genesis 44:14—45:8, the moving story of Joseph making his true identity known to his brothers. Here is an incident which should stir deep feelings. One minister may feel that the story will be too much for his own emotional restraint and will try to tone down the climactic verses. Another may be unimpressed with the emotional content and will concern himself with such things as tone, pronunciation, and pauses. Still another may see in the story a chance to exhibit his elocutionary skill. A fourth may consider the story as a necessary item in the order of service, something to be done and gotten through with, in short, a routine chore. A fifth may be impressed with the wonder of the magnanimity and forgiveness of Joseph, and with the faith that could say, "You meant it to me for evil but God meant it to me for good," and will communicate his own insight and feeling to his hearers as he reads.

Five readers deal with the same passage, yet with what different results! And why? Because of differences in inward attitude and feeling toward what each is to read. One is afraid of the passage. Another thinks only of techniques. Still another sees a chance to show off his dramatic skill. Others may be puzzled, or hurried, or bored, or distracted, or tired to the point of having no enthusiasm in interpreting whatever they read. The inward attitude will always affect the uttered interpretation. Out of the feelings of the heart, the mouth shapes its speech. Adequate appreciation of what one is about to read is the indispensable preface to effective expression, and an eagerness to share that appreciation is the essential postscript for its consummation.

[16] Charles Laughton, "Storytelling," *The Atlantic Monthly,* p. 72.

Chapter 3

The Relation of the Reader to His Audience

It is necessary for the oral reader to assist the listener in comprehending and appreciating what he hears.

LAWRENCE H. MOUAT*

There are three indispensable elements in any act of oral interpretation—the piece of literature, the interpreter, and the audience. Take away any one of these three elements and you cannot have an act of oral interpretation. The concept of literature as something shared, developed in the previous chapter, requires an audience—a person or persons with whom we can share. As also suggested in the previous chapter, literature is created and composed for an audience. The content, arrangement, and style may all have been determined, in part, by the audience to which the author desired to communicate.

Somerset Maugham emphasizes that Burke's style was influenced by his consideration of the audience:

> Of course no one could write at all if he bore these considerations in his conscious mind; the ear does the work. In Burke's case I think it evident that the natural sensibility of the organ was infinitely developed by the exigencies of public speech: even when he wrote only to be read the sound of the spoken phrase was present to him. . . . He

* *Reading Literature Aloud* (New York: Oxford University Press, Inc., 1962), p. 10.

avoided Johnson's faults (small faults to those who, like myself, have a peculiar fondness for Johnson's style) by virtue of his affluent and impetuous fancy and his practice of public speaking.[1]

Not only is the audience necessary to make the act of oral interpretation complete, but the audience also contributes to the act of oral interpretation. The needs of the audience contribute to the interpreter's sense of purpose. Moreover, the audience helps the interpreter empathize with the author, who was also endeavoring to communicate with an audience.

Clifton Fadiman reports his own efforts to help a class of sixteen-year-olds feel what Shakespeare felt:

> . . . we proceeded to read Hamlet fast and superficially, just as the original theatergoers at the Globe listened to it fast and superficially. We tried to re-create in ourselves, by this slapdash method, a little of the wonder, horror, and confusion that that original audience must have felt. We even tried to feel something of what Shakespeare himself may have felt when he wrote the play. By that time the class, or a fair proportion of it, was caught. Then we were in a position to read it all over again, trying to discover what a dozen generations of men have since found in it.[2]

VIEW INTERPRETATION AS A CHANNEL

The interpreter might think of himself as a channel through which the literature moves out to the audience and through which the audience encounters the piece of literature. The channel ought to be deep, free of obstructions, and encouraging to this dual movement. Most oral readers are aware of the danger of allowing their interpretive efforts to impede the flow of literature out to the audience, but unfortunately, not enough readers are sufficiently aware of the equally grave danger of impeding the movement of the audience into the literature.

Jonah is a classic example of a man who saw his role as only that of facilitating the movement of the Word out to the people. He was offended when the people moved in to embrace the Word. The in-

---

[1] Somerset Maugham, *The Vagrant Mood: Six Essays* (Garden City, New York: Doubleday & Company, Inc., 1953), pp. 140-42.

[2] Clifton Fadiman, *Enter Conversing* (Cleveland, Ohio: The World Publishing Company, 1962), pp. 307-8.

terpreter can be just as guilty of self-promotion by intruding himself between the people and their encounter with the selection as he can by intruding himself between the selection and its encounter with the people. A reader's inadequate projection of voice, monotony of rate or vocal melody, and limited expression of mood and attitude may discourage the listener in his endeavor to engage the selection. Encouraging and assisting the listener to hear, comprehend, and appreciate what is being read should be a matter of vital concern to every oral interpreter.

If a reader decided that any enrichment of his oral interpretation with a suggestion of his personal indebtedness to his understanding of God as our heavenly Father, in terms of its redeeming of his own role as a father, would be to intrude himself between the story of the prodigal son and the congregation, he might read it in a detached manner and prevent the congregation from sensing its meaning for human fatherhood.

Paul Tillich suggests the importance of avoiding such an error in interpretation as he discusses the nature of the symbol of God as Father:

> . . . if God is symbolized as "Father," he is brought down to the human relationship of father and child. But at the same time this human relationship is consecrated into a pattern of the divine-human relationship. If "Father" is employed as a symbol for God, fatherhood is seen in its theonomous, sacramental depth.[3]

These points of relationship between the oral interpreter and the audience suggest that the audience is not the peer and critic of the oral reader. Rather the audience is a partner in the act of oral interpretation —an ally, not an enemy. Members of the audience are fellow actors in the drama of interpretation rather than critics preparing devastating reviews to be published in the morning edition.

APPRECIATE THE AUDIENCE

Teachers of oral interpretation are fairly well agreed that if one is to adequately interpret a selection he must appreciate it. An important corollary is that the reader must also appreciate his audience. This appreciation should include not only an awareness of the audience as

[3] Will Herberg, ed., *Four Existentialist Theologians* (Garden City, New York: Doubleday & Company, Inc., 1958), p. 290.

an ally and a partner in the act of interpretation, but also an awareness of the needs, capacities, and moods of various audiences. Such a wide variety of groups is encountered within the church that an appreciation of the audience is a particularly important factor in oral interpretation for religious leaders.

The groups vary in mood or emotional state in a morning worship service, a funeral, a wedding, or a recognition dinner for church-school workers. Church audiences differ in terms of mental alertness and ability to comprehend. A junior high youth group, a young adult Sunday school class, and a congregation at a home for the aged suggest the wide range of mental alertness and ability to comprehend which may confront a church worker. In addition, there is a diversity of needs. A group of Boy Scouts attending Sunday worship services in their open-air chapel may suggest a sharply different set of needs than a group of lay church leaders gathered at a retreat to plan the year's program. Still other needs might be suggested by the congregation meeting in the chapel at the county jail.

Most religious leaders have the opportunity to serve a number of different groups which vary markedly in mood, mental alertness, ability to comprehend, personal needs, and degree of interest. Consequently, they are continually presented with different opportunities to share the gospel. They enrich their sharing by relating their oral interpretation to the specific needs, abilities, moods, and interests of the group to which they are now ministering. Although appreciation of your audience can in no way serve as a substitute for an appreciation of the literature, it is none the less true that you will not reach your full potential for sharing literature until you also fully appreciate your audience.

J. Edward Lantz emphasizes the need for the interpreter to be aware of his listeners as well as aware of his message. "Think of them as you read and be eager to have each one of them comprehend your meaning. Your main reason for reading should be to have them enjoy and understand your interpretation of the author's message." [4]

For the religious leader, oral interpretation should be another way in which he expresses Christian love for his hearers. He should read to them as he would want them to read to him if he were in a similar state of need. In his review of a New York production of Graham Greene's *The Living Room,* Brooks Atkinson indicated how our hearers may react if we fail to read to them "in love."

---

[4] J. Edward Lantz, *Reading the Bible Aloud* (New York: The Macmillan Company, 1959), p. 90.

As a religious drama, *The Living Room* is destitute of love for human kind. It is as ferocious as Cotton Mather. Both T. S. Eliot and Mr. Greene are religious men, but to judge by *The Cocktail Party* and *The Living Room*, they look on the human race with distaste, as if it were a pestilence that infects the earth. There is little joy, peace or compassion in their relation to their people.

In the thirteenth century a theological scholar now known as St. Bonaventura remarked ironically: "Any old woman can love God better than a doctor of theology can." Better also than a modern dramatist with an interest in religious themes. In *The Living Room* Mr. Greene exacerbates not only his characters but also his audiences. Don't look to him for charity.[5]

ASSIST THE LISTENER

Let us consider some of the ways in which the interpreter may assist the audience in its effort to encounter the literature which he is sharing with them.

The interpreter assists his audience when he reads in a manner that enables him to be clearly and easily heard. This means a voice of good quality, amply projected. It also means the use of sharp, distinct articulation.

> It has been well said, that a good articulation is to the ear, what a fair handwriting or a fair type is to the eye. Who has not felt the perplexity of supplying a word, torn away by the seal of a letter; or a dozen syllables of a book, in as many lines, cut off by the carelessness of a binder? The same inconvenience is felt from a similar omission in spoken language; with this additional disadvantage, that we are not at liberty to stop, and spell out the meaning by construction.[6]

In addition to microphones in the pulpits and hearing aids in the pews, we need a genuine concern on the part of religious leaders to assist their hearers by using strong, clear voices and employing good articulation.

Audible and visible clues to the selection's meaning and mood also assist the listener. Softening and hardening of the voice, rising or falling pitch, increasing or decreasing force, quickening or slowing tempo, and

---

[5] Brooks Atkinson, "Graham Greene's Drama About Faith," *The New York Times*, November 28, 1954, Sec. 2, p. x.

[6] Ebenezer Porter, *Porter's Rhetorical Reader* (Andover, Massachusetts: Flagg & Gould, 1831), p. 22.

other audible suggestions all can supply additional indications of the author's meaning and mood. A shrug of the shoulders, a twinkle in the eye, or a general increase in muscle tension may also supply the hearer with significant hints as to the intellectual and emotional content. In normal conversation we communicate as whole persons, supplying our fellow conversationalists with all sorts of audible and visible clues to what we mean and how we feel about it. These clues significantly supplement the words we speak. In oral interpretation we should continue to supply our listeners with a full range of audible and visible clues concerning the meaning and mood of the author.

Too many of us become like the teacher described in *A Lost Paradise*:

> Miss Murphy, who read aloud to us, appeared to be neither interested in nor moved by the McGuffy stories. She read without nuances and exhibited no emotion. Completely indifferent to the music of poetry, she would recite a line like the exquisite "How would I like to go up in a Swing. Up in the air so blue!" in a cold earthbound voice. . . .

We may also assist our audience by our own appreciation of the selection as we interpret it orally. Dr. S. S. Curry emphasizes the importance of giving the listener this sort of aid when we read from the Bible:

> The reading of the Scriptures must never be perfunctory or merely formal. It should not be a mere authoritative presentation of facts or proclamation of words. . . . The reader must live his ideas at the time of utterance. . . . He can manifest to others the impressions made on his own being. But when one soul is made to feel that another soul is hearing a message from the King of kings, he too bows his head and hears the voice of the Infinite speaking in his own breast.[7]

Our own liking for a selection suggests to the congregation that they, too, may encounter in this selection something to like. Beyond a general anticipation, there are opportunities to alert our hearers to portions of the selections which have particular merit through our own eagerness to encounter these words again. What I am proposing would be a suggestion by the interpreter that would act in the margin of the field of attention of the listener. When listening to an orchestra, you may have been helped to anticipate certain parts of the score by the anticipation of the conductor. Perhaps you would find it difficult to recall just what

---

[7] S. S. Curry, *Vocal and Literary Interpretation of the Bible* (New York: The Macmillan Company, 1903), p. 132.

the conductor had done at a given moment. You would probably observe that his action occupied only a few seconds, yet it helped prepare you to appreciate what was coming. In a similar manner, an oral interpreter's appreciation and anticipation of units in his selection may prepare his listeners to more adequately appreciate these units.

The oral interpreter should not plan and execute such anticipation of various portions of his selection. However, if he is fully appreciating his selection and reading it aloud with abandon, such signs of anticipation will occur, and they will provide his listeners with important cues for their own act of appreciation.

RELATE PURPOSE AND CONGREGATION

The audience helps the interpreter clarify his sense of purpose. One of the ways in which the religious leader assists his hearers is to relate his purpose for reading aloud to the particular audience or congregation before him. By so doing, the interpreter may quicken the awareness of his listeners to those aspects of the selection which can be of special interest or help to them.

Remember that the reader's *primary* clue to his purpose will be sought in the literature itself and in a study of the purpose which its author was striving to fulfill; the interpreter surely will not alter this purpose because of needs which his hearers may possess. He will, however, strive to understand and appreciate how the instruction, inspiration, or conversion intended by the author can minister to the needs of his hearers. An analysis of the personal needs of his audience will assist the interpreter in placing a higher value on the author's purpose and will strengthen his desire to share the selection with his hearers because of its relevance for them. Those who pastor, counsel, and minister to others have unique opportunities to learn of deep personal needs; therefore they ought to perceive such relationships more readily.

Keeping before us the long-range potential of the encounter between what we are reading and those who are listening may help us revalue the act of interpretation in which we plan to engage.

HAVE FAITH IN THE AUDIENCE

Finally, the oral interpreter needs to have faith in his audience—a faith like that of Elia Kazan who, in writing about his projected work with the Lincoln Center Repertory Company, declares: "We work in the confidence that people will respond to live goings-on and that audiences are looking for something meaningful. The final faith of any artist must be that if a thing is meaningful and alive to him, it will prove so to others." [8]

---

[8] Elia Kazan, "Theatre: New Stages, New Plays, New Actors," *The New York Times Magazine,* September 23, 1962, p. 29.

Chapter 4

The Relation of the Reader to the Act of Reading Aloud

He who not only understands fully what he is reading, but is earnestly occupying his mind with the matter of it, will be likely to read as if he understood it, and thus, to make others understand it; and in like manner, with a view to the impressiveness of delivery, he who not only feels it, but is exclusively absorbed with that feeling, will be likely to read as if he felt it, and to communicate the impression to his hearers.

RICHARD WHATELY*

The degree to which one can understand, feel, and concentrate on such understanding and feeling as he reads a selection aloud depends, in no small measure, on the relationship he feels to the act of reading aloud.

DOMINATED BY THE READING SITUATION

Many readers feel dominated by the reading situation. When they begin to read aloud they feel that they must meet certain standards of pronunciation, grouping of words, rate of reading, and previously determined patterns of vocal melody. Sometimes such feelings are prompted

* *Elements of Rhetoric* (Boston: James Monroe and Company, 1844), pp. 269-70.

by earlier instruction in reading when they were required to read against a stop watch, an evaluation chart dealing with pronunciation, or a marked copy of a selection. In other cases the reader may have chosen to view the act of reading aloud as a pursuit of perfection in vocal mechanics, substituting this view for the more troublesome consideration of whether he is really communicating to his hearers.

Whatever the reason, it is most unfortunate if the reader feels dominated by a demand for perfection in vocal mechanics. Such a view diverts him from the meaning of the selection, masks the real desires of his auditors by focusing on their imagined expectations, and inhibits his presentation. Whately warns that an interpreter's reading will not be communicative "if he is occupied with the thought of what their opinion will be of his reading, and, how his voice ought to be regulated; if, in short, he is thinking of himself, and, of course, in the same degree, abstracting his attention from that which ought to occupy it exclusively." [1] This view is also inadequate, as it fails to allow for any participation on the part of the audience. It does not take into account the manner in which the audience assists the interpreter in his work. The reader does not need to communicate the meaning and feeling perfectly. Rather, the interpreter should sufficiently launch the thought and feeling in the mind and heart of the listener so that the listener will be prompted to develop them further.

Another way in which readers may feel dominated by the reading situation is the notion that they must observe a definite restraint in reading. Whereas the previous view gave the audience too little credit for its part in the act of oral interpretation, this view gives the audience too much credit. Examine this advice to the reader of the liturgy:

> . . . liturgical prayers . . . ought to be recited without emphasis and in a level tone, the enunciation distinct and clear but the rate somewhat faster and the voice more subdued than ordinary reading requires, the intention being to create an atmosphere of devotion and to provide a background of prayer, rather than attempting to force individual aspirations into a prescribed form or pretend to cover the complete exercise of prayer.[2]

If the reader were to follow this advice, he would find himself denied the use of emphasis and variety in tone, and would be compelled to

---

[1] Richard Whately, *Elements of Rhetoric* (Boston: James Monroe and Company, 1844), p. 270.

[2] *The Order of Divine Service for Public Worship* (London: Oxford University Press, 1919), pp. 4-5.

read at a rapid rate and in a subdued voice. Moreover, it is suggested that the reader is to be part of a "background" rather than a leader of worship. Many religious leaders still adhere to this or similar advice, not only in the reading of prayers, but in the reading of all parts of the liturgy. They feel compelled to maintain a definite amount of restraint in their reading.

An oral interpreter dominated by a view of leading worship that denies him the use of natural abandon in reading is severely handicapped in his effort to communicate the meaning and the mood of his selection. It is unlikely that he will be able to provide sufficient suggestions of thought or feeling to stimulate the members of the audience to complete these suggestions in their own minds. The seriousness of this handicap can be more fully appreciated when we consider Dr. Curry's comments about the reading of prayers:

> Prayer is always suggestive and subjective. As the noblest aspiration of the soul, it calls for the most spiritual modulation of the voice and the deepest unity of all the elements of naturalness. The outward test of whether the man is praying or not is shown by vocal expression, for prayer is an attitude of soul.[3]

Readers who are dominated by either of these attitudes are not likely to achieve the freedom or naturalness in reading aloud which would make for full and genuine communication of thought and feeling; they are prevented from reading as though the word read from the printed page were the same as the spoken word.

BOUND BY DUTY

Somewhat more fortunate is the reader who has chosen to relate to the act of reading aloud as he would to a duty to be performed. He does not feel dominated by the act, but neither does he feel a maximum freedom of expression in it. He tries to handle the assignment well and has a sense of competence about it. However, the satisfaction he has afterward is that of a job well done. The difference between this view and the feeling of being dominated by the task lies in the area of how one feels the task must be done. The reader who feels the assignment as a duty is more concerned about the satisfactory completion of the

[3] S. S. Curry, *Vocal and Literary Interpretation of the Bible* (New York: The Macmillan Company, 1903), p. 6.

whole task than anxious about doing the task in a specific way. As P. E. Sangster remarks, "We tend to read the Scriptures as merely a necessary part of a service, conscious as we do that the congregation has heard it all before and is not listening very accurately." [4]

If a religious leader suddenly realizes that he is reading merely because this is his appointed task, or that he reads passages from the Bible mechanically without really thinking of their meaning, he needs to ask himself if the reading of the worship service has become just another chore. Again, if he discovers that he frequently has started the congregation praying without being in prayer himself, he needs to ask if leading in prayer is only another duty to be performed.

Let it be clear that there is more hope for good oral interpretation with this attitude than in a relationship where one feels dominated by the task of reading aloud, for in seeking to fulfill the duty the reader may still read in a natural manner and utilize abandon in expression. He is apt to have more enthusiasm for undertaking a task in which he does not feel regimented in terms of how he may do his work. Moreover, if he actually considers it a duty, he is likely to feel some obligation to prepare well and to meet minimum standards in leadership.

FREED AND EMPOWERED TO SHARE

However, the reader who views the reading task as an activity which frees him and empowers him to share spiritual treasures with his hearers is the one most likely to communicate when he reads aloud.

For this reader the Bible and liturgical materials, the congregation, and the service of worship do not repress expression—instead they stimulate and encourage it. The words that accompany the presentation of the Bible at a coronation in England suggest how this reader thinks of the Scriptures: "the most valuable thing this world affords. Here is wisdom, this is the royal law. These are the lively oracles of God." [5]

With George Morrison he marks the wonder, the miracle, and the living power of the Scriptures: "It is a living power in kinship with

[4] P. E. Sangster, *Speech in the Pulpit* (New York: Philosophical Library, 1958), p. 60.

[5] *Ibid.*, pp. 60-61.

the heavens. I think of all the men that it has helped, I think of all the women it has blessed. I think of the weeping eyes it has dried, and of all the broken hearts it has comforted."[6] Like Charles Laughton, the Bible is not dull for him. He has discovered that people not only like to hear it read aloud but that they will ask for more.

The reader who finds the reading task to be an activity of sharing in which he enjoys both freedom and strength of expression will read prayers and thanksgivings as the genuine sentiment of his own mind at the moment of utterance. His praise of God will have dignity, but it will also be vital and from the heart, intending to quicken the emotion rather than to give information or theological analysis. In adoration of God his spirit will surge Godward. His eagerness to share the riches of the liturgy will evidence his conviction that "the church is a religious institution and makes its greatest contribution when it is a worship center."[7]

This reader also expects that the congregation will endeavor to complete his suggestion of meaning and mood. He believes that as he struggles to serve the Word of God to them they will also strive to take and eat. He believes that if he reads well the people will be moved to attend, understand, and reflect on its entire meaning.

These possible relationships to the act of reading aloud suggest that the reader would do well to bear in mind the parable of the talents. Those who choose to be dominated by the task can be compared to the servant who buried his talent in the ground because he knew his lord to be a hard man. Those who view public reading as a duty may be compared to the servant who earned two talents to return with the two entrusted to him. The servant who traded his talents and made five more may be likened to the reader who views the reading task as an endeavor in which he finds himself freed and empowered to share the spiritual riches of the worship service.

Now it is probably true that most of us cannot be accurately identified as maintaining any one of these relationships exclusively; we may waver back and forth among all three. However, most of us drift far too heavily toward the feelings of domination and duty.

---

[6] *The Greatest Sermons of George H. Morrison* (New York: Harper & Row, Publishers, 1959), p. 126.

[7] Gerald Kennedy, *His Word Through Preaching* (New York: Harper & Row, Publishers, 1947), p. 21.

EMBRACED AS AN OPPORTUNITY

Instead we ought to eagerly embrace the opportunity to read aloud, with the expectation that one day the following words will describe our own reading of the Scripture.

> He opened the book as a skilled interpreter of its deeper meaning. He made clear its rich content by the very manner of his reading. He uncovered to the souls of men the divine message which lay beneath the surface of the written word by his own intelligent, sympathetic modulation. He showed its bearing upon present need and duty. He related its agelong helpfulness to the moods and opportunity of the hour.[8]

Finally, let it be clear that these remarks are not intended in any sense to endorse exhibitionism or self-gratification through reading aloud in the church. They are intended to disturb the great majority of us who are poor stewards of the opportunity to share the gospel through oral interpretation and to encourage us to a more adventuresome participation in the act of reading aloud.

---

[8] Charles Reynolds Brown, *The Art of Preaching* (New York: The Macmillan Company, 1922), p. 204.

Chapter 5

General Preparation for Reading Aloud

However familiar a man may be with the Scripture, however able to command himself in an emergency, so as to read a few words or a short lesson, no conscientious minister who understands the nature of vocal expression will allow himself to neglect the thorough preparation of the lesson he is to read. He may have studied it thoroughly years before, but he knows that this is not enough. There must be a present readiness, a freshness of thought and feeling.

S. S. Curry*

Lack of adequate preparation accounts for more bad reading in the church than any other factor. Moreover, most religious leaders frequently admit to not having prepared adequately. Indeed, so many admit to poor preparation that one begins to suspect that they feel they have set the matter right by confessing their failure.

REASONS FOR INADEQUATE PREPARATION

Some say that they are hesitant to spend much time in preparation because they fear that if the selection is too familiar they will read it poorly. They point out that too much review can cause the reader to

---

* *Vocal and Literary Interpretation of the Bible* (New York: The Macmillan Company, 1903), p. 294.

lose interest and consequently his reading becomes matter-of-fact. Others state that the material is already written, and thus one does not need to spend as much time in preparation. After all, he does not have to compose it, he only needs to read it aloud. Those who adhere to the belief that the reading should be restrained and provide a kind of "background" for the worshipers might be wary of preparation, fearing that it would lead to "dramatic" reading, with the reader imposing too much of his interpretation on his listeners. Many who read sermons from manuscript as well as prayers of their own composition seem to regard their work in composing the manuscript as adequate preparation for reading it aloud. Tom Wicker's analysis of "Kennedy as a Public Speakah" suggests that this viewpoint is open to question:

> Mr. Kennedy's personal preparations were casual . . . he underlined some phrases for importance and made some markings to guide his delivery; with an eye to the television camera, he also read a page aloud. . . .
>
> The President eschewed rehearsals. . . . He did not plan or practice gestures or memorize a line. . . .
>
> In delivering the State of the Union message, however, Mr. Kennedy read some passages as uncertainly as if he were seeing the text for the first time. In others, he sounded like a court clerk calling cases. . . .
>
> At the University of Washington in Seattle, he delivered a beautifully written speech warning that there were no quick "American solutions" to Berlin and other problems. Mr. Kennedy droned through his text as if he were an uninterested teacher cramming *Paradise Lost* down the throats of equally uninterested students.[1]

Another group guilty of faulty preparation are those religious leaders who so procrastinate in the selection or composition of the materials which they will read aloud that no time remains for preparing to read them well.

However, most of the people who fail to make adequate preparation for reading aloud probably do so because they have no definite approach to preparation in which they have confidence or which assures them of a satisfactory stage of readiness for reading aloud. Consequently, the following pages will be devoted to helping you work out a satisfactory method of preparing yourself to do a competent job of oral interpretation. Let us begin by asking what a satisfactory plan of preparation should do for the reader.

---

[1] Tom Wicker, "Mr. Kennedy as a Public Speakah," *The New York Times Magazine,* February 25, 1962, pp. 70-71.

AIMS OF PREPARATION

There are five basic aims which any method of preparation should help the oral interpreter achieve. First, it should help the reader become informed about the character of the selection—its sources, relevance to its age, editorial modifications, and so forth. Second, it should assist the reader in his effort to appreciate the literary style of the selection—its form, mood, and total impact. Third, it should help the reader sense the application of the thought to his own soul and experience the feeling in his own heart. Fourth, it should quicken the reader's awareness of the relevance of the thought to the needs of his listeners. Finally, the method of preparation should increase his competence to communicate the thought and feeling through his vocal expression and bodily action.

BENEFITS OF A REGULAR METHOD

To begin our discussion of principles to be followed in developing a method of preparation, we will consider the benefits of following a similar method or plan for each preparation. When one subjects himself to this discipline he finds that he is able to get down to business sooner. He develops habit of inquiry and reflection which can be set into action promptly. Regular preparation procedure helps the reader develop skills in preparation. The more he works with the various parts of this method, the more efficient and adept he becomes in the use of them.

An equally important merit of a standard approach is that it can be evaluated, corrected, and improved. If a procedure is not making any significant contribution, it can be altered or a different procedure can be substituted for it.

Still another benefit of following a regular plan is that it can be readily adapted to special situations; some steps could be omitted and others substituted. A casual, unstructured approach is difficult to alter or adjust because one is not sure what it is that can be altered.

Finally, the regular plan of preparation, faithfully followed, demands less and less attention from the reader. When he is familiar with his plan of preparation and adept in its use, he has more freedom to understand and appreciate his selection.

Consequently, the discussion in the remainder of the chapter will assume that the reader is following a regular procedure for each preparation to read aloud. In his book *Reading the Bible Aloud,* J. Edward Lantz provides a two page Preparation Form which the reader is to fill out for each reading.[2]

PRINCIPLES OF PREPARATION

The following principles are intended to serve as a guide for you as you formulate your own plan of preparation for reading aloud. In later chapters specific plans will be suggested for preparing to read particular portions of a worship service. Now you are asked to consider principles for constructing such a plan.

1. Space your preparation with sufficient time intervals to encourage reflection and assimilation. The oral interpreter needs more than a passing acquaintance with the character of a piece and more than a sudden infatuation with its literary style. His knowledge and appreciation of a selection need to mature and ripen so that they come to full fruition at the moment he is to interpret the selection to his audience.

2. Read the selection frequently and in a variety of ways. Scan the selection to get an overview. Read it slowly and carefully, noting ideas, words, phrases, figures, and punctuation. The rapid rate at which we normally read a poem fails to stimulate imagery. However, the more reflective approach of aesthetic appreciation allows us to summon up a wider array of images. Dwelling on a phrase or line may evoke all sorts of images, which in turn widens the range of our reactions. Read the selection briskly, feeling for its progression and moment of climax. Read it aloud to yourself and listen to words, sounds, and to the rhythm of the selection. Read it aloud to another person and concentrate on sharing the selection with your listener.

3. Feed your mind steadily with information about the nature and content of the selection and about its literary type and its particular style. Repeated stimulation of the mind with information about the piece increases the possibility of feeding the mind at a moment when it is particularly assimilative or appreciative. This principle assumes that the first principle will be followed and that preparation will be spaced. Professor Simon also explains the merit of this procedure in preparation:

---

[2] J. Edward Lantz, *Reading the Bible Aloud* (New York: The Macmillan Company, 1959), pp. 49-51.

> The more one knows about the particular work of art, the richer the appreciation. The life of the author, his background or experience, the spirit and nature of the times during which he lived and wrote; the background of the poem or story, style, prosody, and allusions; all these give a richness of appreciation, an understanding and responsiveness that cannot be had without them. The more ideas associated with any selection, the more stimulation to response, the more ways in which the whole man may react.[3]

4. Consult other works of art which have been inspired by this piece of literature. Painting, sculpture, music, poetry, and fiction inspired by Biblical passages represent rich possibilities for providing us with images, sounds, and associations which will quicken our understanding and appreciation. When preparing to read the story of the prodigal son, for example, we might well find our appreciation enlivened by viewing Rembrandt's "Return of the Prodigal Son." As V. Loevinson-Lessing, Deputy Director of the Hermitage State Museum in Leningrad, observes, "The picture is effective in its understanding of how to express in simple, monumental forms the mastery and strength of love." [4]

The help that you may find in such a religious painting is suggested by Professor Bailey's description of his viewing of Raphael's Sistine Madonna.

> In 1895 I first entered the room in Dresden where is hung Raphael's Sistine Madonna. Before it a crowd of people were sitting in silence, eyes fastened upon that face which suggests the mystery of motherhood, sense of participation with God in creation and salvation, and the inability of a mortal to comprehend a role so sublime. To understand such a picture is to have a religious experience.[5]

Or we might turn to the work of a contemporary poet, Tony Stoneburner, entitled "Harvest of the Heart," for further quickening of our appreciation of the Biblical narrative of the prodigal son:

> O Lord my God, I was a prodigal.
> I thought MY HEART IS HUSK UPON A TALL
> CORNSTALK IN TORN-BY-FALL-AND-WINTER SHOCK.

---

[3] Clarence T. Simon, "Appreciation in Reading," *The Quarterly Journal of Speech,* XVI, No. 2 (1930), 190.

[4] "Most Popular Paintings in Eight Museums," *The New York Times Magazine,* March 18, 1962, p. 36.

[5] Albert Edward Bailey, ed., *The Arts and Religion* (New York: The Macmillan Company, 1944), p. 12.

I thought THE CORE, THE BEST OF IT, HAS FED
THE BEAST WITHIN THE STALL TO KEEP HIM STILL.
I thought THE COB-AND-HUSK, THE REST OF IT,
IS FODDER (FARMERS DO NOT EVEN STORE
IT IN A CRIB BUT LEAVE IT FOR THE WIND
TO SHAKE APART, OR FEATHER, IN THE WET-
AND-SNOWY WEATHER). As I think I talk,
I told to thee, O Lord my God, I thought
MY HEART IS HUSK, until thy hurt-but-not-
hurt-hardened-to-a-leather hand had hold
of it, an ear of nubbin corn, and with
a country art did shuck the wrapper off
to show the hidden glory of the gold
of nugget kernels,
O THY HAND, UNCALLOUSED, IN THE COLD.

A reading of Stoneburner's work might assist the interpreter to achieve the third aim of preparation, namely, a sense of the application of the thought to his own soul and an assimilation of the feeling into his own heart.

The novel, too, can serve as a means of quickening the reader's appreciation of passages that he desires to read. A reading of Thomas Mann's *Joseph in Egypt* would be helpful preparation for an oral interpretation of the Biblical narrative on which it is based. Similarly, the chapter entitled "The Sermon" in Herman Melville's *Moby Dick* would enliven a reader's appreciation of the book of Jonah.

The recitatives in such musical works as Handel's *Messiah* and Haydn's *Creation* can also stimulate a reader in his preparation for orally interpreting the Scriptures. Often described as "singing speech" or "speaking song," recitatives suggest how the oral interpreter may tackle particular problems of interpretation. The way in which the soloist treats the word *comfort* in "Comfort Ye, Comfort Ye My People" (from *The Messiah*) may help the oral reader in producing the sound and feeling of comfort. (Although the recitative has been specifically mentioned, oratorios, anthems, hymns, and other musical compositions are also strongly recommended as stimulants to the reader's appreciation and imagination.)

Likewise, drama can make significant contributions to the oral interpreter's sharing of his selection. From a *Passion Play* to *J. B.*, drama can illustrate vivid plot, characters, setting, and mood.

The dance should also be considered. Interpretations of the Lord's

Prayer and the Twenty-Third Psalm express feeling, and particularly the degree of feeling. Progression of thought and the point and intensity of climax are dramatically emphasized through movement and posture.

Biblical passages have been used in these suggestions, but the suggestions hold good for other kinds of literature too, and there are many more possibilities for stimulating one's understanding and appreciation through consulting the arts than it has been possible to indicate in this brief treatment.

5. Think of the selection you are to interpret in terms of its potential meaning for particular persons in the audience. In his report on a West Coast poetry festival, Jack Gilbert indicates that this approach would be particularly germane when preparing to interpret contemporary poetry:

> If no clear direction in American poetry emerged at the festival it is because there is none yet. Some material has been added to the case against the too moderating influence on the academy and there is evidence that, through default in high places, poetry is needed more urgently than ever as a source, not merely of delight but of perspective, taking over from philosophy the function of changing our lives.[6]

Equally emphatic and more inclusive are the assertions of August Heckscher (Special Consultant on the Arts to the White House):

> In all these vast, sometimes half understood enterprises, the arts are bound to play a crucial role. They alone can humanize the great community of tomorrow, can provide a focus for the free days and years of the new leisure, can interpret and make meaningful the areas which science opens up. The outward scene must be brought in the end into at least a rough conformity with the values which the arts foster and encourage.[7]

When the worship leader contemplates the potential power to change lives which is contained in the portions of the service which he will read aloud, and when he thinks of this power being released in the lives of particular persons, then he has a stimulus to understanding, appreciation, and expression which will move him to excellence in interpretation. A pastoral concern to relate the hearer and the gospel can make a tremendous contribution to interpretative ability.

---

[6] Jack Gilbert, "Between Verses: Report on a West Coast Poetry Festival," *The New York Times Book Review,* September 9, 1962, p. 34.

[7] August Heckscher, "The Nation's Culture: New Age for the Arts, *The New York Times Magazine,* September 23, 1962, pp. 15, 39.

In addition, such an approach may assist his hearers to give an appreciative ear to his interpretation. When the members of the congregation sense that the interpreter is eager to have them understand and appreciate the service, they become eager to have such appreciation and understanding. The feeling that the leader cares about how one personally participates in worship is a powerful stimulant to one's reception of those points of the service which are interpreted orally.

6. Read the selection aloud several times with the aim of improving your *oral* interpretation of it. During these oral readings you will want to achieve adequate projection of voice as well as improve your ability to suggest meaning and mood through vocal color and tone.

> In all good literature the general sound of a poem or passage corresponds with the mood in which it is written. One of the first things a reader must do is to look for the correspondence between mood and sound; for the quiet hushed words that speak of tranquility, for the light phrases of gaiety, for the full sonorous noisy words of battle and tumult, and for the long, slow-footed rhythm of grief and lamentation.[8]

During this period of oral practice the reader will also want to improve his timing. He should be concerned with rhythm, the placement and use of pauses, the duration of vowel sounds, and similar matters. The reader should note places where he could support his vocal effort through eye contact with the congregation and become particularly familiar with key passages so that he can utilize eye contact to help convey their meaning. He will also want to give some attention to his body. He should practice a comfortable, alert stance with his head erect. Once again Professor Porter's words indicate the merit of this sort of concern on the part of the reader.

> In some few instances, I have observed the head to be kept so erect, as to give the air of haughtiness, in others it is dropped so low, that the man seems to be carelessly surveying his own person. In others, it is reclined towards one shoulder, so as to give the appearance of languor or indolence.[9]

---

[8] John T. Marshman, "Art Approach to Reading Aloud," *The Quarterly Journal of Speech*, XXXVII, No. 1 (1951), p. 37.

[9] Ebenezer Porter, *The Rhetorical Reader* (Andover, Mass.: Flagg and Gould, 1831), p. 68.

7. Just prior to the reading of the selection for the audience, seek to renew your understanding and appreciation of the selection. A renewal of the thought and mood of the literature immediately before reading it aloud may ward off a sense of vagueness or staleness. It may also serve as a "warm up" and stimulate more spontaneity of expression.

These seven principles of preparation will assist you in developing your own plan of preparation for the act of oral interpretation. They are intended to provide minimum coverage of the essential matters. In later chapters the application of these principles will be considered in relation to specific reading tasks.

Remember that the plan of preparation which you develop ought to help you meet the goals set forth earlier in this chapter. Moreover, the plan should be one you can regularly employ—it ought to be practical. Finally, you should constantly evaluate and perfect your plan so that your preparation will improve and your plan adjust to your developing skills and your growing understanding of the art of oral interpretation.

PART TWO: THE ACT OF ORAL INTERPRETATION

Chapter 6

The Use of the Voice in Oral Reading

Three things only are required to make a good reader. He must read so that what he reads shall, in the first place, be heard; in the second, that it shall be understood; and, in the third, that it shall be felt.

JOHN PIERPONT*

At first glance you may have thought that the above quotation was an odd choice for opening a discussion on the use of the voice. However, on rereading you will notice that it places the necessity of being heard first. The use of the voice is just as indispensable to having your interpretation understood and felt as it is to having your interpretation heard. Vocal emphasis and rise and fall in pitch can suggest the word which is important; it can suggest whether we have a question or a statement of fact. The sound of your voice may indicate that you are serious or that you speak in jest.

---

* *The National Reader* (Boston: Carter, Hendee, and Co., 1833), p. iv.

RESTRAINT UPON VOCAL FREEDOM

If the voice is to be used effectively in oral interpretation, it must be free to respond to the content of the selection. The voice should spontaneously respond to the thought and mood being expressed. Three kinds of restraint to such vocal freedom may be experienced by the reader.

Psychological Restraint

Most readers think that they are doing a better job than they actually are. They feel that they must hold a tight rein on their projection of voice, rise and fall of pitch, and variations in vocal quality to avoid the accusation of being "too dramatic." This feeling is not the result of conceit but of an untrained ear—they evaluate their reading in terms of the way they sound to themselves. Instead, they should evaluate their reading in terms of how it sounds to the members of their audience.

Oral interpreters might well alter the words of Robert Burns to read, "Oh would the gift some power give us/ to hear ourselves as others hear us." The oral interpreter has to continuously train his ear to hear himself as others hear him. He must develop an "audience ear." Leonard Wibberley's description of Big Sister Elizabeth reading *Treasure Island* aloud to his class suggests that she possessed and used an "audience ear."

> I can see her now . . . describing how Billy Bones told Jim Hawkins to keep a weather eye open "for a sea-faring man with one leg." She was capable of wonderful modulations of her voice. When blind Pew came tapping with his stick down the frosty road to the Admiral Benbow Inn, with his band of cutthroats about him, I could hear the sharp rap of his stick on the frozen surface, and feel the terror of his approach . . . and when it came to the wicked chorus of:
>
> Fifteen men on the dead man's chest
> Yo ho ho, and a bottle of rum
>
> Big Sister Elizabeth gave out with such gusto that one would have thought, as Stevenson put it, her voice had been "tuned and broken at the capstan bars." [1]

---

[1] Leonard Wibberley, "Father's Adventures in Reading Aloud," *The New York Times Book Review,* November 13, 1960, p. 1.

As oral readers we have to recognize that we cannot content ourselves with what sounds adequate to us. We must work to produce a voice which will sound adequate to our hearers. Our question should be: "How do I sound to the fellow on the aisle in the third row under the balcony or the lady half way back on the left side with the restless youngster beside her?

Most of us have trouble in maintaining continuous evaluation of our voice with an "audience ear" because we think of good speaking and good reading as possessing the speech characteristics of lively conversation. Our problem arises from our conversational habit of evaluating our vocal production in terms of how we sound to ourselves. In conversation we are in such close proximity to our hearers that it seems unnecessary to be asking ourselves how we sound to them. We can simply ask, "How do I sound to myself?" By and large this is an adequate method for conversation. However, this method is totally inadequate for public reading.

Unless we have learned that when we sound a certain way to ourselves we sound quite another way to others—unless we have developed an "audience ear"—we are in no position to evaluate our presentation by listening to ourselves as we read aloud in public.

Until we really learn to meet the auditory needs of others, rather than simply to satisfy our own auditory preferences, we face a severe psychological restraint of our vocal freedom—for vocal freedom is the freedom to use whatever vocal effort is necessary to make what we read be heard, understood, and felt by our listeners.

Biological Restraint

A second serious vocal restraint which readers experience is biological in nature. A sign of such restraint is the Adam's apple (voice box) drawn up tight under the chin. Other signs are a tense, strained sound in the voice, a ragged edge on the voice (such as one may hear when a person is very fatigued), or a sense of tightness in the throat centered around the Adam's apple. Biological restraint affects the quality of the voice, its strength or force, and the pitch range.

Before we go further, it would be well to make certain that we have a common understanding of these three terms. Dr. James Rush in *The Philosophy of the Human Voice* defined *pitch* as follows.

> The term *pitch* is applied to the variations of tunable sound, between its lowest and its highest degree. This variation between gravity and acuteness is represented in the human voice by the two extremes of hoarseness and screaming. The different degrees of pitch in music are denoted by what is called the scale. . . .[2]

For our purposes we shall consider pitch as the movement of the voice up and down the musical scale. We may speak of a high pitch in a first tenor range or of a low pitch in a base range.

Dr. Rush reminds us that when we speak about the *quality* of the voice we are talking about the kind of voice it is. Quality may be commonly described in some of the following terms: harsh, hoarse, rough, smooth, full, thin, meagre, tight, gravelly. It is probably the quality that we rely on most heavily to identify a voice as belonging to a particular person.[3]

When referring to *force,* think of both loudness and body, of both carrying power and weight, of both projection and strength. Dr. Rush notes that the force of a voice is often described with such words as loud, soft, strong, and weak.[4]

Having a better understanding about the terms pitch, quality, and force, let us turn to a consideration of the causes of biological restraint of vocal expression. Biological restraint of the voice indicated by a tight throat may be due to one of several failures in voice production.

1. The reader may fail to breathe deeply and fully and therefore lack sufficient breath to produce an adequate voice without a tightening of the vocal cords. If only a limited supply of breath is being directed up through the voice box (larynx), the vocal cords must tighten in order to vibrate adequately to produce the amount of voice desired. As a result, the inadequate breath supply causes the throat to tense in order to produce adequate vocal projection and the voice becomes restrained.

2. The reader may fail to direct his breath through the voice box with adequate force. It is possible to have an ample supply of breath but to direct it through the voice box in such a weak or lethargic manner that the vocal cords must still tighten in order to deliver an adequate voice. If you will pause in your reading and pant like a

---

[2] James Rush, *The Philosophy of the Human Voice* (Philadelphia: J. B. Lippincott & Co., 1859), p. 71.

[3] *Ibid.*, p. 201.

[4] *Ibid.*, p. 385.

dog, or count cadence, you will be able to feel the diaphragm moving in and out at about the level of your belt. Such action of the diaphragm is needed in order to thrust the breath up through the voice box with sufficient force to allow the vocal cords to remain relaxed and still vibrate in an adequate way to produce the strength of voice desired.

3. The reader may fail to keep the throat (voice box) open and relaxed. It is possible to habituate speaking from the throat with a tight, tense larynx. Then, even though the reader has an adequate supply of breath and uses the diaphragm to thrust the breath up through the voice box, he will not have good vocal quality nor will he have his full natural pitch range available to him. Vocal restraint will be experienced primarily in terms of pitch and quality and, in a lesser degree, in terms of force. At this point stop your reading for a moment and execute a good, healthy yawn. Now yawn a second time and notice how open the throat feels. If you have adequate breath support for your vocalizing, the throat should feel just as open when producing a strong voice.

If your throat tightens up while you are reading aloud in public, there are two ways to relax and open the throat again. One is to swallow. Men can look in a mirror, deliberately tighten up their throats, and then swallow. They will see the "Adam's Apple" drop back down into a relaxed position. It is also possible to open the throat up by sighing. Both of these methods (swallowing and sighing) can be inaudible and relatively invisible, so that the reader can employ them during the act of reading aloud in public.

4. The reader may fail to place his vocal production forward in his mouth toward his teeth. Some readers produce the voice in the back of the mouth because they are trying to pitch their voices lower. The placement of the voice is achieved by restricting the vocalized exhalation at a particular place in the mouth and causing head resonance to be more pronounced in that area. Those who place their voice in the back of the mouth tend to tighten their throat and lower the soft palate to trap the voice there, while those who place the voice forward direct the breath stream against the hard palate which forms the roof of the front of the mouth. Well-meaning listeners frequently tell a religious leader that he ought to speak in a lower pitch. When a speaker tries to choke back or partially swallow his voice in order to produce a voice which has a lower pitch, he so seriously affects the quality of his voice that any change in pitch is more than offset by undesirable effects in quality; these bad effects

are due to the tensing of the throat and voice box which results from this unnatural method for obtaining a lower pitch. Other readers may find that their failure to place the voice forward in their mouths is due primarily to a lethargic way of speaking.

In brief review, the reader may develop the vocal freedom vital to effective oral interpretation by maintaining an adequate breath supply, utilizing the diaphragm to push this breath supply up through the vocal cords, keeping the throat relaxed and open, and placing the voice forward in the mouth. The key is the ability to produce a voice of adequate strength while the throat remains relaxed and open (rather than tensed and tight); in this way he will overcome the biological restraint of vocal expression.

Artistic Restraint

A third type of vocal restraint which affects all but the most able readers is the restraint imposed by artistic inability. A leader of worship may genuinely want to provide the sort of oral leadership which is deemed helpful by his congregation, and he may also have developed some good habits of voice production—yet when he calls the congregation to prayer he says *Let us pray* with an ascending pitch and declining force so that his congregation hears a timid question, *Let us pray?* It sounds as though he is asking the congregation, "Should we do this now?" Such a leader would need help in developing better control of the pitch and the force of his voice, so that he could say to the congregation *Let us pray:* or *Let us pray.* or *Let us pray!* rather than seeming to ask *Let us pray?* Even though the leader has the desire and adequate vocal resources, he still needs the ability to deliver the voice at the pitch and with the force that is needed to properly interpret the summons to prayer.

Artistic inability frequently leads to a self-imposed restraint by the reader who does not attempt to fulfill his desire to be adequately heard by his audience because he doubts his ability to give the thought sufficient expression. This is particularly true if some special problem in interpretation presents itself. His inclination is to play it safe and not risk an effort at oral interpretation which may cause him to stumble or go awry.

We shall now consider some ways in which disciplined use of pitch, quality, and force can contribute to one's artistic ability and give him more freedom of vocal expression.

PITCH

Level of Pitch

Let us begin with a consideration of a few of the possibilities presented by the use of pitch. First let us think of pitch and its contribution to expression in the use of a single word. A number of different meanings or moods can be given to the word *oh* by using a different pitch or pitch pattern.

1. Rising pitch: *oh* ⟶ surprise
2. Falling pitch: *oh* ⟶ disappointment
3. Constant pitch: *oh* ⟶ concern
4. Upward arc: *oh* ⟶ pleasure
5. Downward arc: *oh* ⟶ pain

These movements in pitch are frequently identified as a *pitch glide* because the change is continuous with no break.

In a series of words another kind of pitch change known as the *step* can be easily employed. If one wished to make an emphatic denial or refusal he might step the pitch down on a repetition of the word *No.*

No
No
No
No

On the other hand, if one wanted to make emphatic an affirmation or acceptance he might step the pitch up while repeatedly speaking the word *Yes.*

Yes
Yes
Yes

In this case the pitch change occurs between words rather than during the words as in the glide.

In addition to the pitch glide and the pitch step there is the matter of melody. This term describes the patterns of pitch—the vocal movement up and down the scale—which the reader employs. When someone speaks of a ministerial tone he would probably be more accurate if he spoke of ministerial melody. One frequently occurring pattern is an ascending pitch reaching its peak at about two-thirds of the way through the sentence and then declining through the remainder of the sentence. A series of sentences could be diagrammed as follows:

Certain melodic patterns are typical of certain situations. If an old friend stops at our home to pay an unexpected call, we would be able to hear in sentences like the following a melody that helps express the pleasure of the occasion. "Well, hello! My, it's good to see you. You're looking fine. Come on in and see the family." You will probably find that the voice tends toward the higher pitch level and that the ends of sentences rise in pitch or stay at approximately the same pitch level as the preceding part of the sentence. Also, the movements in pitch will most likely be made in a glide rather than in a step.

As a musician is always on the alert for a melody that may come from the street, the park, the factory, or the store, so the oral interpreter needs to be constantly on the alert for speech melodies that may be heard in everyday conversations, in casual speeches, and in formal addresses on important occasions. If you develop a keen ear for speech melodies, you will be more able to recreate them and use them in oral interpretation.

Ralph Dennis, formerly Dean of Northwestern University's School of Speech, used this approach for his own work in oral interpretation.

> . . . He told that he had built the pattern of his dialect for the leading character in *The Melting Pot,* by Zangwell, on a fragment of a sentence he had heard a man say when he passed a group of immigrant workmen sitting on a curb eating their lunch the day after the sinking of an excursion boat, *The Eastland,* in the Chicago River. The man had said, "I see by the paper ____________." The melody of that line haunted Dennis. He kept saying it to himself. Later when he developed the character in *The Melting Pot,* he used the melody on a single line he chose from the play as a "key" line, "God never curses so utterly but that he leaves something to dance with." Keeping the dialect consistent throughout was accomplished by checking back to these two lines.[5]

[5] Edna Gilbert, "Teaching Interpretation: Students Recall Methods of Early Leaders," *The Speech Teacher,* November 1962, p. 295.

Pitch is also a key item when the reader wishes to suggest how the speech of a person in his selection would sound. While quality is the most important factor in suggesting vocal personality, pitch is also helpful in aiding the hearer to differentiate between the voices of two characters. This is particularly true if there is a difference in the age or sex of the characters.

Lack of Variety in Pitch

If you suspect that you do not achieve sufficient variety in pitch, there are several things you might do.

1. Be certain that you are making full use of your optimum pitch range. This is that range on the musical scale where you can produce your longest, strongest, clearest tones with the greatest ease. If you cannot secure the help of a choir director or speech teacher, then starting at middle C on the piano, sustain tones (Ho-o-o-o) up and down the scale (one and a half to two octaves) noting where you sustain the longest, strongest, clearest tones with the greatest ease. During your efforts to locate your optimum pitch range you might bear in mind that the tendency is to pitch the voice too high. Making full use of your optimum pitch range will stimulate more variety in pitch.
2. In order to exercise your speaking voice in producing various pitches you might speak the words of the Doxology and the Gloria, approximating the melody pattern to which they are sung in the worship service. Concentrate on "stepping" your voice up and down in pitch vigorously, in accord with the melody.
3. As you hear vocal melody in various speech situations, mimic these melodies until you can reproduce them accurately.
4. As you are moved to make changes in pitch, make these changes in an exaggerated manner while practicing the selection you plan to read aloud—overdo so that you think you've jumped too high or too low. Frequently you will discover that instead of sounding overdone, it actually sounds more natural. Exaggeration is sometimes the way to freedom in expression.

QUALITY

Quality is extremely important because it is a way of suggesting more subtle meanings. It pertains not only to *what,* but also to *how* we mean and to what degree. Closely related to the emotions, it is frequently regarded as a clue to its producer's personality. Anderson reminds us that quality "is one of the most subtle forms of emphasis and the most difficult to control . . . its control is dependent upon a delicate and intricate co-ordination and adjustment of virtually the entire mechanism involved in speech." [6]

Difficult as it may be for the reader to produce particular kinds of vocal quality and control them, there are still aspects of quality which he can produce, control, and utilize to advantage in oral interpretation.

He can make his voice sound hard or soft. The hard voice can be achieved by firm support of the voice and vigorous, precise attack and termination of consonant sounds. By contrast, the softer voice has a more relaxed support of tone and more moderate and less definite attack and termination of consonant sounds. A heavy voice can be suggested by use of a lower pitch range and a very deliberate rate, whereas a voice can be given the characteristics of lightness by moving to a higher pitch level and reading more rapidly.

The bold voice requires definiteness of emphasis, forceful projection, and general abandon. The timid voice, on the other hand, can be suggested by uncertainty of emphasis, limited projection, and general restraint.

Remember, however, that a full understanding and a genuine appreciation of the selection to be read plus a healthy, trained vocal mechanism are vital prerequisites to any effort to adjust or alter vocal quality.

Precisely because quality is important in suggesting the more subtle meanings and moods, every oral reader must constantly work to improve this aspect of his voice. As an oral interpreter you will be heartened by Anderson's advice for developing this aspect of your reading voice:

> Read aloud. . . . Choose your material carefully so that a variety of definite attitudes and purposes are represented . . . material to which you can and do react in a positive and vigorous manner. Awaken your responses, make an effort to get the author's purpose and point of view, and allow these to dominate completely your interpretation. If these requirements are conscientiously met, oral reading will be . . . of inestimable value in the development of desirable vocal quality.[7]

[6] Virgil A. Anderson, *Training the Speaking Voice* (New York: Oxford University Press, Inc., 1942), pp. 175-76.

[7] *Ibid.*, p. 177.

FORCE

The oral interpreter employs force to clarify meaning and to indicate mood or feeling. Failure to place emphasis on the proper syllable of a word will confuse your hearer as to the word's meaning. You can imagine the difficulty the congregation had when the preacher prayed "save us from our ad*ver*sary" instead of "save us from our *ad*versary."

By emphasizing different words in a phrase you can alter its meaning. The meaning of "*What* is truth?" is something quite different from "What is *truth?*" Vocal force may pertain to syllables, words, phrases, or entire sentences.

Professor Akin attempts to underscore the importance of the application of force for the communication of meaning by discussing *sense stress*. "Sense stress is the stress put on syllables and words to emphasize a certain meaning and to express an important idea more forcefully. In ordinary factual speech, each syllable will be stressed or not stressed according to the fact that is being presented." [8]

The degree of vocal force can also suggest distance, boldness, certainty, and various other moods. The proximity of an auditor in a play or dialogue may be suggested by the force of voice. Whether an opinion is stated secretly or openly may also be indicated by the degree of vocal force. A forceful voice is associated, too, with such moods as anger and fear. Great joy, as well, might be expressed with a forceful voice.

Three faults in the application of force are common among religious leaders. The first is the failure to make any marked application of force. Their public reading is characterized by a restraint of force which makes their reading seem bland, even lethargic, and which provides few if any clues to those parts of the selection which are intended to be emphatic. The second fault is the development of a habitual pattern of emphasis. Frequently this pattern is one in which the first part of each sentence is emphasized and thereafter the force of voice declines rapidly. The difficulty here is that the reader's em-

---

[8] Johynne Akin, *And So We Speak: Voice and Articulation* (Englewood Cliffs, N.J.: Prentice Hall, Inc., 1958), p. 211.

phasis is often in conflict with the author's intended emphasis, and the listener is left with the confusing task of separating the author's meaning from the reader's interpretation. In addition, a habitual pattern of emphasis produces a monotony of force which dampens the listener's attentiveness.

In terms of the over-all use of force, the need to use a voice which can easily be heard by all your listeners has already been emphasized. Let us now add that the strength of voice must increase as the listener fatigues. Frequently the opposite is true. Many readers maintain a strong projection for the first third of the reading and then gradually fade, so that by the concluding sentence their reading is lifeless and close to inaudible.

A third fault which, in the minds of some critics, deserves to be ranked with the first two (if not above them) is the forceful vocal projection of some moods and the restrained underprojection of others. Religious leaders frequently give full vocal support to a mood of earnest seriousness and barely make audible the lighter, humorous mood or the mood of joy. A good many readers, after careful analysis, will probably discover that in terms of force of voice they have a few moods that they favor and several that they slight.

COMPLIMENTARY COMPONENTS

Finally, let us note that in any interpretive effort, pitch, force, and quality are blended to provide a total impression. A good part of the time the adjustment of these three components occurs spontaneously, without any conscious effort by the reader. Usually if a reader makes a definite emphasis in force, involuntary adjustments will also take place in the pitch and quality of his voice. Consequently it should be kept in mind that although the previous discussion focused on these three elements individually and dealt with them in isolation, in actuality they affect one another as complementary components contributing to a single vocal act.

As we endeavor to use our voice more adequately to interpret the meaning and mood of what we are reading aloud, let us be encouraged by Dr. Curry's description of the rich potential of the voice for the truthful presentation of thought:

The importance of this vocal part of language to the truthful presentation of thought cannot be overestimated. Man's inflections and tones will be believed more readily than words. The reason for this is that verbal expression manifests not only the conscious feelings, but also the unconscious emotions and conditions of the speaker's character and soul, and is recognized and read by the instincts of man.[9]

[9] S. S. Curry, *The Province of Expression* (Boston: School of Expression, 1891), p. 55.

Chapter 7

The Use of the Body in Oral Reading

The more the reader can respond by appropriate movements—the more he can bring the muscles of the hands, arms, legs, trunk, and face into the complex of movements—the more vivid will be his emotional experience and the more completely will he get the significance of the particular bit of literature which he is reading. No one can fully appreciate while his body is inert and lifeless.

CLARENCE T. SIMON*

In this chapter we will consider how the interpreter's use of bodily action can help him more adequately interpret the selection and help his hearers appreciate it more fully.

BODILY ACTION AIDS INTERPRETATION

As the opening quotation suggests, the use of bodily action may facilitate the reader's fuller appreciation of what he is reading. His use of bodily action may help the reader feel more in the selection. Bodily action may also stimulate appreciative responses by other parts of the body. If the reader allows his appreciation to be expressed

* "Appreciation in Reading," *The Quarterly Journal of Speech,* XVI, 2 (1930), p. 190.

through bodily action, he makes a total appreciative response to his selection more probable.

BODILY ACTION AFFECTS VOICE PRODUCTION

An erect posture is an important factor in breathing for oral interpretation. If the reader's shoulders are allowed to slump forward and in, they will inhibit the expansion of the chest and thereby limit the amount of breath available for voice production. Such a limitation of breath supply, in turn, adversely affects the quality and projection of voice. The interpreter's rate of reading may also become more mechanical and less natural. It is not inconceivable that the reader may even be forced to group words in a manner that conflicts with meaning because he does not have a sufficient reserve of breath to handle longer groupings.

Equally important to the voice production needed for oral interpretation is a relaxed, open throat. Tuck your chin down sharply until it touches your throat. Note the sensation of tenseness in the larynx. Now tilt your head way back until it seems that the back of your head is touching your shoulder blades. Again note the sensation of tightness in the larynx. Next, turn your head sharply to the right and then around 180 degrees to the left. In each instance give attention to the restriction placed on the movement of the larynx. Just to demonstrate to yourself that the position of the head does affect the larynx and its functioning, again assume each of the positions previously described and attempt a full, wide open yawn. You will quickly discover that you cannot execute a full yawn in any of these positions. Now assume each of these four positions again and attempt to swallow. With equal rapidity you will discover that you cannot swallow either.

The position of the head which allows for the optimum of relaxation in the larynx is somewhere between these four extremes. The head held erect in an alert but relaxed manner with the chin in line with the buttons of the shirt is a good position. In this position you will be able to swallow and yawn with ease. Try it.

If one desires to look sharply either to the right or left, he should turn his whole body in that direction so that he does not turn his head at an extreme angle. Likewise, if the manuscript is so far below his line of vision that he must dip his chin down, he ought to raise the reading stand or hold the copy in his hand at a good reading level so that he can avoid choking off his voice.

At all times the reader should so control the posture and movement of his head that an optimum degree of relaxation and openness of throat is possible, for a relaxed, open throat is vital to maximum vocal participation in the act of interpretation.

Bodily action can also aid the reader in achieving abandon in expression. Bodily action, such as a gesture involving the hand and arm or a walk from one point to another, encourages abandon in vocal expression because it provides a more natural climate for such abandon. Usually when a person is engaged in an animated conversation his animation can be observed in bodily action as well as in vocal expression. If an interpreter attempts to achieve animated vocal expression while maintaining an inactive or even rigid posture, he is trying to produce vocal animation in an unnatural bodily context. Consequently, such expression will be more difficult to achieve.

Another important effect which the use of bodily action has on voice production is that of supporting the vocal interpretation. When vocal effort is accompanied by an effort in bodily action, the vocal effort normally becomes more intense; this occurs because the reader has more of a feeling that his whole being is engaged in the interpretative act.

The reader may also find that the use of bodily action helps him to perfect his timing. Any contribution which bodily action makes to the reader's appreciation of the selection should improve his sense of timing as he attempts to interpret the selection orally. In addition, a reader may be able to gauge the duration of a pause by the time it takes him to move from one spot to another on the platform or by bringing the arm and hand into position to execute a gesture. Or if two characters are conversing and the reader employs slight changes in posture to indicate which character is speaking, the time required to make these changes may help the reader provide the appropriate intervals of silence between the speeches.

The interpreter's over-all posture may assist him to communicate the rhythm which is appropriate to the selection. A greater degree of casualness in posture may help a reader communicate a slow, easy going mood. An erect, alert posture may help one communicate the mood of brisk efficiency.

By way of brief review, let us now recall that bodily action can aid the oral reader in several ways. First, it can facilitate the reader's fuller appreciation of what he is reading. Second, breathing for oral interpretation can be helped or hindered by the posture which the reader maintains. Third, optimum vocal relaxation which provides for maximum vocal expression is dependent on the posture of the neck and head. Fourth, bodily action may also act as a stimulant or encouragement to abandon in vocal expression. Last, bodily action may help the interpreter in the matter of timing—with pauses as well as with the rhythm of the selection.

BODILY ACTION AIDS LISTENER APPRECIATION

Bodily action may serve as a visual aid for the listener. He may see a transition as well as hear it. In the facial expression and muscle tone of the reader he may see a mood of sorrow as well as hear it expressed in words and voice.

The listener will find it easier to appreciate the characters who are speaking when the reader suggests the nature of the characters through bodily action. As soon as the listener has identified certain traits of bodily action with each character, he can more readily discern which character is speaking. When a dialogue is being read aloud, this advantage of visual as well as vocal clues to the identity of the person who is speaking will help the hearer instantly identify the person and thereby improve his comprehension of the selection. We need to remember that bodily action helps to gain and hold the listener's attention. It commands attention because it is a visual stimulus and because it involves movement.

Every oral interpreter must realize that he has an even greater need to help his hearer attend to what he is reading than does the public speaker because oral reading tends to be less direct and less personal than extemporaneous speaking, and therefore does not command our attention as readily. Any listener who falters in his attention to the act of oral interpretation is limited in his appreciation of the selection. This limitation is in direct proportion to the degree of his inattention. Consequently, the oral interpreter who gains and holds the attention of his listeners contributes directly to their ability to appreciate the selection. If bodily action had only the merit of helping your listeners attend to your public reading, it would be well worth any effort required to become skilled in its use.

TYPES OF BODILY ACTION

The first type of bodily action which the oral interpreter may employ is that of muscle tone or tension. Muscle tension or tone may range in degree on a continuum from relaxed indifference to keyed-up alertness to the tautness of muscles produced by fatigue, anxiety, or fear. Even when no large bodily movements are made—no gestures of head or arms and hands—the audience will still perceive signs of the degree of tension. Some of these signs may appear in our facial expression, the position and activity of our fingers, our stance, and sometimes in the position and amount of mobility in our shoulders.

Not only can listeners discern the amount of tension involved in our interpretative act, but they can also detect the kind of tension. There is a tension that may be motivated by eagerness and there is another tension motivated by anxiety. There is a relaxation of laughter and good humor and there is also a relaxation that may come from exhaustion. Again, the eyes, the shoulders, the stance, and the hands provide the telling clues. The degree of control which the reader exercises over his bodily action may be another important clue to the kind of tension which the leader is seeking to communicate.

A second type of bodily action employed by public readers is their stance (the way they stand before their audience). A reader can stand before an audience in a bold or in a reluctant manner. His stance can suggest fatigue, determination, casualness, or any other attitude. Consequently the stance which a reader takes can suggest the attitude of the author or of persons in the selection who are speaking. When the reader senses that even his stance is involved in this interpretative act, he will be well on the way to an adequate use of bodily action.

After observing that "Most of us fail to realize the extent to which we preach with our bodies," Bishop Kennedy suggests this goal for standing before a congregation:

> A preacher ought to be able to stand before people and give the impression of perfect control over his whole body, or better yet, to give the impression that every muscle is the servant of the message.[1]

---

[1] Gerald Kennedy, *His Word Through Preaching* (New York: Harper & Row, Publishers, 1947), p. 73.

Movement of the head is a third type of bodily action which the oral interpreter may utilize. One may hang his head in shame, hold it high in pride, bow it in prayer, thrust it forward in determination, shake it in denial, nod it in approval, turn it to the side as if examining something from another angle, and draw it back in apprehension. Head gestures have the same implications in public speech that they do in conversation.

Closely allied with the movement of the head is the movement of the shoulders. Movement of the head and shoulders are often combined in one over-all gesture. Drooping shoulders may suggest weariness. One shoulder thrust forward may imply a move forward. Shoulders leaning forward may suggest a desire for a more personal communication. The shoulders can be shrugged to say "I don't know" or to shrug something off. The shoulders can also be significant in an effort to suggest the person whose description or words appear in the selection that the reader is interpreting.

Now we come to the part of the body that is usually thought of when gesture or bodily action is mentioned—the hand and arm. Gestures by hand and arm can be used to describe, to emphasize, and to express mood and attitude.

The oral interpreter may be somewhat limited in the use of his hands and arms for gesture due to his need to handle the material from which he is reading. He would be well advised to devise methods for handling his materials which allow his hands to be free a considerable part of the time for use in gesture.

Hand gestures are used with such frequency and variety in conversation that they may serve as indicators, showing whether we really are free to communicate with our whole person and whether we have sufficient skill and control to allow us to function naturally.

STANDARDS OF GOOD BODILY ACTION

All bodily action should be motivated by the reader's response to the selection which he is interpreting. It should help the interpreter more fully appreciate his selection. Bodily action should communicate the material for which it is serving as a visible symbol. (If it suggests something different to the auditor, it is a hindrance to communication.)

Bodily action should also be appropriate to the occasion and the situation. Lastly, it should help the audience attend to your reading and appreciate the meaning of your selection.

FREEDOM TO USE BODILY ACTION

This chapter is not intended to suggest that bodily action ought to be employed for its own sake. Neither is it intended to imply that bodily action can be substituted for a thorough knowledge and appreciation of the selection to be read. The meaning of this chapter is that you need to become free to use bodily action in interpretative reading. Indeed, you cannot possibly realize your fullest potential as an oral interpreter until you have real freedom to use bodily action in your interpretative efforts.

The kind and amount of action used varies greatly, depending on the nature of the selection, the personalities of interpreters, the kinds of audiences, and the physical surroundings in which interpreters work. The point is not kind or amount, but the freedom to use action when it is appropriate, meaningful, and helpful to you and your audience as you participate in the interpretative act.

Freedom to use bodily action may be developed by studying your selection and noticing where certain kinds of action could contribute to your appreciation and expression. Then in your oral practices attempt to use the intended action at the designated places in the selection. After you have broken the ice with this rather mechanical approach so that the use of action no longer seems strange and awkward, you will find it happening in a spontaneous and creative manner as you are interpreting your selection.

Dr. Simon describes this method with regard to posture:

> Assuming the posture of emotion, with its consequent muscle tensions, increases the vividness and vigor which the reaction will sweep through the reader. At first this will have to be done consciously; undoubtedly it will be done clumsily. But as skill increases, the adjustments become more subtle and accurate, and ere long the student actually has increased the keenness and vigor of his presentation.[2]

[2] Clarence T. Simon, "Appreciation in Reading," *The Quarterly Journal of Speech,* XVI, No. 2 (1930), p. 189.

To appreciate your selection more fully, interpret it more adequately, and communicate it more completely—become free to use bodily action when reading aloud. Work for abandon in the use of muscle tone, stance, head, shoulders, arms, and hands. Remember that action is itself communication through visible symbols.

Chapter 8

The Use of the Eyes in Oral Reading

The intercourse of soul between speaker and hearers is carried on more unequivocally through the eye than in any other way.

EBENEZER PORTER*

The very first matter that the oral interpreter must settle in regard to eye contact is whether he intends to use it and, if so, to what extent. If the reader decides not to look at his audience when he reads aloud to them, he should seriously consider the extreme limitation which he is placing on his communicative potential; he must compensate for this limitation through use of voice and bodily action. He should plan to make use of any composure gained by keeping his eyes fixed on the page to achieve more abandon in expression through voice and bodily action.

Even with very strong compensations, the reader should realize that he cannot match the rapport which would be possible if his communication included the use of his eyes. Dr. Curry aptly expresses this point in his *Province of Expression:*

> There are three kinds of expression, one belonging to the eye and ear, one to the ear alone, and one to the eye alone. . . . A look of the

---

* *The Rhetorical Reader* (Andover, Massachusetts: Flagg and Gould, 1831), p. 67.

> eye, a grasp of the hand may speak what many sentences would fail to convey. In the stir of deep feeling, when the tongue is dumb with inadequacy to express the depths of the soul of man, the lip trembles, the eye flashes, the body expands, the hand is held out and gives a gentle pressure, and all is clear; the soul at once feels the links of empathy, the appreciation of the whole situation.
>
> It is evidently the intention of nature that the language of each part bear witness in its proper sphere to the truth expressed by the others, and thus "in the mouth of two or three witnesses every word is established." Without this harmonious coordination of languages, without this harmony of all nature's intended agents of expression, perfect truthfulness and adequacy of expression are impossible.[1]

Finally, the reader should understand that he will be presenting his material in a manner contrary to the preference of the audience. Martin Cobin's experimental study yielded quantitative data supporting the following conclusion. "The present study established audience preference for a reader's maintenance of good eye contact in a face to face situation."[2]

FAMILIARITY WITH THE SELECTION

If, in the light of the foregoing observations, you decide to look at your hearers and communicate with them through eye contact, then two kinds of familiarity with your selection are vital to the implementing of your decision:

1. You need to know the selection and to know about the selection in all the detail and completeness that has been suggested in earlier chapters. The selection should seem like home ground, familiar territory, and friendly country. No reader will feel comfortable in looking away from the selection to the audience if the material he is reading seems strange or alien territory.

2. You must know the way your selection has been set down on the particular page from which you are reading. You must know that when you look down to begin the next paragraph you will find it one-third of the way down the page. Or you should know that the sentence you are reading is continued at the top of the next page

---

[1] S. S. Curry, *The Province of Expression* (Boston: School of Expression, 1841), pp. 56-57.

[2] Martin Cobin, "Response to Eye Contact," *The Quarterly Journal of Speech,* XLVIII, No. 4 (1962), p. 418.

and is concluded by an exclamation point. You should know where you may encounter a somewhat different sentence construction or even a different spelling than you might find in other printings. The pages from which you are reading should be like a familiar map which you have used many times and on which you can quickly identify points and readily discover your own position.

COMPETENCE TO MEET EYES

In addition to being familiar with his selection, the reader must be competent to meet the eyes of his listeners and communicate with them during this meeting of eyes. He will find it helpful to look into the eyes of one individual at a time. Eye contact will be more meaningful if the reader can continue to look at a single individual for a sufficient period of time to gain attention, emphasize a point, or even observe some indication of a response. The amount of time spent in eye contact with various listeners will be affected by several factors including the degree of rapport, the effectiveness of your communication, listener responsiveness, and the mood or meaning which you may be trying to communicate.

In order to overcome their hesitation to look listeners squarely in the eye, some readers prefer beginning with the toughest pair of eyes in the audience—the most apathetic, aloof, or critical eyes. Such readers feel that once you have settled things with these eyes, the rest are easy. Other readers prefer to start with the more friendly, interested, appreciative eyes and, after gaining encouragement from them, move on to deal with the more difficult eyes.

Either of these methods has merit and you should employ the one that appears as though it would be most helpful to you. The important thing is that you begin with a definite pair of eyes and then, systematically working your way through your audience, try to look as many persons in the eye as possible.

COMMUNICATION WITH THE EYES

A wife can warn her husband with a quick glance across the dinner table that a subject should not be discussed further in the presence of the children. With a single glance an interviewer can tell the personnel manager that a prospective employee did not score well on an aptitude test. A young lover can look across a crowded room and, with the expression of his eyes alone, say to his beloved, "I love you."

When the oral reader looks at his audience, he is observing them and seeking their attention, but he is also doing something infinitely more important. He is communicating the meaning and the mood of the selection which he is reading aloud.

It is most important that the reader realize that his eyes are as much a part of his communicative act as is his voice. The reader needs to be conscious of saying to his audience with his eyes that he desires to communicate directly with them, that he is concerned about how they are receiving his communication, and that the selection moves him to communicate certain meanings and moods.

The primary use for the eyes in oral reading is not to observe accurately what is on the printed page, important as that may be. Rather it is to communicate the meaning and mood of the selection. Every reader needs to be vividly aware of the act of expressing his interpretation through the medium of eye contact with his hearers. More than this, he needs to attempt frank and full expression through the use of his eyes. Not until the reader has experienced real abandon in the use of his eyes will be be fully aware of the rich contribution which the expression in one's eyes can make to the act of oral interpretation.

The reader should utilize ocular expression as a means of stimulating expression in his other features. As the reader senses that his efforts to communicate meaning through eye contact are, in fact, resulting in a more lively and extensive facial expressiveness, he will be encouraged to pursue the development of his ability to interpret meaning and mood with his eyes. As Quintillian observed, "the face is what is most expressive . . . it is often equivalent in expressiveness to what can be said in many words." [3]

The reader never really enters into the area of genuine competence in the use of ocular expression until he is able to appreciate the full effect which his interpretive efforts are having on his hearers. Only as the reader is able to accurately observe the appreciative responses of his audience is he able to enter fully into the use of eye contact and to adequately accompany oral expression with ocular expression.

Mrs. Theresa K. More, professional children's storyteller for the

[3] Quintillian, *Institutes of the Orator* (London: B. Low, 1744) II, 327.

Newark Public Library, gives a good description of such an experience. "When you see the children's faces and watch their response, the rapture in their upturned eyes, you know you're not just telling a tale, you're giving of yourself, you're sharing the beauty and the truth with the children." [4]

In summary, the reader may improve his competence to communicate with his eyes by realizing that his eyes play an important role in communicating the meaning and the mood of his selection. He needs to be aware that their expressive function is more important than their observing function. He may utilize ocular expression as a means of stimulating general facial expression. Observation of the fuller appreciation which his hearers have for the selection as a result of his use of his eyes should encourage him to make more effective use of eye contact to communicate the ideas and feelings suggested by his selection.

ADDITIONAL SUGGESTIONS

In order to develop greater freedom to utilize his eyes in the interpretive function, the reader may find it profitable to read through his selection looking for those sections which would be particularly aided by the expression of the eyes. Then, as he reads the selection aloud, he should make a special effort to utilize eye contact at these points. For this purpose a mental note rather than a written note is preferable. Mental notes are less likely to produce a mechanical presentation and more likely to be adjusted or altered in the light of the needs and demands of the immediate reading situation.

The reader may also find clues for appropriate use of ocular expression in the response of the rest of his body to a unit in the selection. Expression of the eyes is always a part of the total gesture or posture; the entering of the body into certain postures and gestures will frequently be a good indicator that eye contact should be utilized as well. For instance, if you should find yourself leaning forward toward the audience and your right index finger pointing directly at the audience, then you will probably discover that usually your eyes ought to be engaging the audience also.

The freedom for the eyes to move readily away from and back

---

[4] Elizabeth McFadden, "Story Teller Enjoys Job," *Newark Sunday News*, December 30, 1962, Sec. 7, p. R-3.

to the text is aided by proper lighting and correct distance of the text from the eyes. The very least which a reader can do is to make certain of good light and a reading stand of proper height. Failure to do so may make it necessary for the eyes to be primarily involved in the task of following the text. Clear copy in a serviceable binding is also an important contributor to such freedom. Every minister who has attempted to read from a "pocket ritual" printed on very thin paper at a committal service in a cemetery on a cloudy, windy day would surely emphasize the importance of this last suggestion.

RHYTHM OF OBSERVATION AND COMMUNICATION

There are some striking similarities between the use of the breathing mechanism for voice production and the use of the eyes for the expression of the meaning and mood of a selection. Breathing is a biological function by which we keep the body supplied with oxygen. We make use of the exhalation part of this function to produce voice. When speaking we shorten the inhalation phase and lengthen the exhalation phase. Exhalation is also more forceful than in ordinary breathing.

Likewise, one uses his eyes quite differently in silent reading than he does in oral reading. In oral reading the eyes must quickly view the words on the page; then, as the words are vocalized, the eyes are employed to express the meaning and mood of these words.

As speech is imposed on the function of breathing, so ocular expression is imposed on the function of seeing. As we noted earlier, the rhythm of breathing changes for speech with shorter periods for inhalation and longer periods for exhalation. In a like manner, the oral interpreter must shorten the periods when he views the page and lengthen the periods when he looks out to the audience. A rhythm of viewing the page and then looking at the audience must be developed so that there is artistic coordination of silent reading and visible expression.

Even with the development of a reading-interpreting rhythm the reader will still exercise some degree of control over this rhythm and adapt it to special interpretive problems. As he nears the climax of a mood or a point of major emphasis, he may want even more freedom from the printed page in order to employ ocular expression of mood or to give added emphasis to the delivery of a unit by maintaining a direct eye contact with his auditors.

No oral reader will find it adequate to occasionally look at the audience or to plan to look at the audience for a few words at particular points in the text. Only an appropriate rhythm of reading and expression will give the interpreter the recurring freedom from copy which makes full abandon in interpretation possible.

There is a third phase of this rhythm of reading and expression. In one sense it can be considered a part of the reading act. However, it is such an important factor in oral interpretation that it warrants special consideration. After the words have been read, the reader must appreciate them. Except for sight readings, his prior preparation will enable the reader to experience this appreciation almost instantaneously. In addition, his intense concentration and quickened senses will facilitate the speedy impression of what he is reading on his mind and feelings. The reader must always be certain that this appreciation phase is not slighted or bypassed, for none of the suggestions that have been made for the use of the eyes will be to any avail if the reader skimps or omits this appreciation phase. Without the motivation of the appreciation experience ocular expression will be mechanical and meaningless.

At this point, too, our analogy with the process of breathing for speech can be pressed. The intake of breath may be adequate and the time ratio between inhalation and exhalation may be good, but if there is no adequate control of the exhalation phase, then the voice may still be poorly produced. Likewise, the words may be accurately read and the proportion of the cycle allowed for ocular expression may be adequate, but if the expression is not adequately controlled by the reader's appreciation, the interpretation will be poorly expressed. So the oral interpreter's rhythm can be thought of in three phases: reading, appreciation, and expression. The expression phase should be motivated and controlled by the appreciation phase; therefore the latter must not be slighted.

Cox summed up our plan for the use of the expressive potential of the eyes in reading aloud when he wrote:

> Your eyes must not be ever on the page; they should turn continually from the page to the audience. This is an art that requires some practice to learn. You read at a glance, with vastly more speed than you can speak an entire sentence, or some complete part of a sentence. This

the mind seizes and retains sufficiently to enable you to remove the eye from the book and speak the words from a momentary memory of them, while your eyes are upon the audience. I can not too earnestly impress upon you the importance of this process. The efficiency of your reading depends upon the more or less of ease with which you accomplish it, and therefore, you can not devote too much pain to its acquisition.[5]

[5] Edward W. Cox, *The Arts of Writing, Reading, and Speaking* (London: Horace Cox, 1911), p. 182.

Chapter 9

The Use of Time in Oral Reading

Hurry, hurry, is the greatest enemy of literary appreciation and enjoyment.

S. H. CLARK*

In this chapter we will consider the factor of time from several perspectives. We will think of it first as a means of more accurately communicating the meaning of the selection being read. We will also survey some of the ways in which time affects the comprehension and appreciation of the audience. We will investigate the relationship of time to the general skill of the interpreter. Finally, attention will be given to allied subjects such as grouping, centering, and rhythm.

When the reader uses the pause to indicate the way words are to be grouped—"Almighty God (*pause*) Father of Our Lord Jesus Christ" —he is employing time to indicate meaning. Again, when the oral interpreter increases the duration of a syllable within a word such as C-O-*M*fort, or when he quickens or slows the pace of his reading to emphasize a key passage, he is using time to communicate meaning.

The way in which the oral reader handles time influences the ease with which listeners hear and understand his interpretation. For one thing, poor use of time can result in reading which is too rapid,

---

* *Interpretation of the Printed Page* (Chicago: Row Peterson & Co., 1915), p. 247.

jerky, or singsong. All three of these characteristics interfere with an auditor's attention and appreciation.

The reader, too, is affected by his timing as he reads. As indicated in the previous chapter, if a reader proceeds too rapidly he denies himself an adequate opportunity to appreciate the selection. He also makes articulation and expression more difficult because the more rapidly reading is attempted the higher the degree of coordination required. Even the problem of alternately reading from the text and then looking at the audience is aggravated by a rate that is too rapid for the ability of the reader.

RATE OF READING

These observations lead us to the formulation of a principle regarding the use of time in oral interpretation. The reader's basic rate of reading and its variations should represent a composite judgment of the rate suggestive of the meaning to be communicated, the rate which enables the audience to best appreciate the selection, and the ability of the reader to employ a particular rate. This principle emphatically denies that there is a fixed rate at which any given selection should be read or at which any particular reader should read. It further denies that there is any fixed rate for optimum audience appreciation and comprehension. It affirms the necessity for making a specific judgment for each situation and the necessity of adjusting this judgment during the act of oral interpretation. The need to continuously adjust the rate and its accompanying variations arises from the dynamic character of literature, of the reader, and of the audience.

Literature is a living, not a dead art. Good literature deals with themes, affairs, truths, and beauties that are eternal. Its power to affect our own understanding is virtually unlimited. A piece of literature may provide new insights and new pleasures long after it has become familiar to us. Some passages of literature seem to provide new insight or pleasure with each reading. To say that there is one rate at which a piece of literature should be read is to deny the dynamic, living, suggestive potential of literature, and the possibility that in our next encounter it will say something different to us which will affect the speed at which we should express its meaning to others.

Surely every reader knows that such factors as prior practice, degree of fatigue, poise, and general health affect his optimum speed for the act of oral interpretation. It is sheer folly for him to attempt to read at a previously determined rate if his personal condition on this occasion prevents him from reading effectively at that particular speed. Attempting to read at a rate which is not easily manageable destroys the naturalness and spontaneity of one's reading. Many readers find that the rate at which they can read effectively may alter during a reading and adjustment of the rate is necessary at that time.

As listeners, we also know that the speed at which we can receive and comprehend the read word varies with the degree of our interest and attention, our familiarity with the material being read, and the extent of our response to the reading. We also know that these conditions may change during the course of the reading.

Consequently the rate at which you read a selection aloud should be the result of a composite judgment representing the rate which will best suggest the meaning of the selection, the rate at which the reader experiences the most naturalness of expression, and the rate which makes for greatest ease of listening for the audience. Moreover, the rate which was deemed best and utilized during practice readings may need to be altered as these three factors are appraised during actual public reading of the selection. The judgment should be continuously made as the selection is read and the rate altered accordingly.

THE PAUSE

After the reader determines his basic rate, he must consider the other time factors which contribute to communication. The pause is one factor which most readers could employ more effectively. Harrison Karr described the pause as one of the most useful instruments of vocal expression. He also advised, "Especially should persons who read manuscripts and secretary reports learn this factor of pausing. It will make their reading sound more like speaking; it will add meaning and significance." [1]

The oral interpreter can use the pause in many ways. As suggested earlier, the pause serves, in part, as the listener's clue to punctuation. The reader may pause briefly before and after a subordinate clause to set it apart from the rest of the sentence. He may pause for a longer period to indicate to the listener that the sentence is complete. The

[1] Harrison M. Karr, *Your Speaking Voice* (Glendale, California: Griffin-Paterson Publishing Co., 1938), p. 77.

pause he uses to set one paragraph apart from another is likely to be of a still longer duration. Pauses of varying lengths may also be used to indicate other kinds of grammatical units.

In his discussion of the grammatical pause Dr. Curry wrote,

> It shows the connection of ideas. For example, in Luke 2:16 where the shepherds are spoken of as finding "Mary and Joseph, ( ) and the babe lying in a manger" if no pause be read before the reference to the child, the lying in the manger may apply to all three.[2]

In addition to separating units of thought, the pause can also be utilized for emphasis. It may precede, and emphasize through the suggestion of anticipation. A pause following the word or phrase may make it emphatic by suggesting that it is worth pondering. These emphatic pauses give the listener an opportunity to respond more fully to what has preceded or to what will follow the pause.

The preceding discussion suggested several purposes for the use of pauses. The importance of making purposive rather than mechanical use of pauses is emphasized by Kathern Taylor Loesch's study of the prosodic patterns in the poetry of Dylan Thomas. Concluding a detailed study of six poems she wrote, "In none did pause appear to be metrically required at the line ends." [3]

Byron W. King reminds us of four purposes for the use of pauses:

> *First.* The pauses are for the purpose of making the ideas distinct. . . . *Second.* Any change of words from their natural order, demands a pause. . . . *Third.* Pauses are needed for any omission of words or ideas. This gives the auditors time to supply such words or ideas. . . . *Fourth.* There are pauses for emotion. . . . As a principle, it will be observed, the greater the emotion the more frequent and longer the pauses.[4]

DURATION OR LENGTH

Another important way of using time to communicate is to vary the length of single sounds. When reading a phrase from a prayer such as

[2] S. S. Curry, *Vocal and Literary Interpretation of the Bible* (New York: The Macmillan Company, 1903), p. 147.

[3] *Speech Monographs,* XXIX, No. 2 (1962), p. 112.

[4] Byron W. King, *Practice of Speech* (Columbus, Ohio: Wm. M. Wikoff, 1888), pp. 88-89.

"all we, like sheep, have gone astray," the meaning of the word *all* is affected by the length of the vowel sound. If the duration of the vowel is brief, then the word may imply or suggest many or most. Whereas, if the vowel is stretched out the word will suggest that every one of us is included. Or again, how the reader handles the first vowel in the word *patient* when he reads "love is patient" may well suggest the difference between seven times and seventy times seven.

Duration of sounds also communicates feeling and mood. Many pastors fail to indicate the deep and genuine affection implied in the words "Dearly beloved" because they have not thought of how the duration of certain sounds in these words could more fully communicate a pastoral affection for their people.

Thompson and Fessenden voice a warning about the matter of duration which all religious leaders would do well to heed:

> Many readers, it should be emphasized, cannot depend upon their normal speech habits. By giving too little time to vowels they produce a nervous, jerky effect, and by clipping consonants they suggest poor speech environment, interfere with clarity, and impair the pleasantness of their voices.[5]

GROUPING AND CENTERING

Grouping and centering will also assist the reader in improving his timing. In grouping, two matters are important.

1. The words must be grouped according to meaning and thought units. A word belonging to one thought should not be grouped with words belonging to another thought. The meaning is changed considerably if one groups "Is not this Jesus—the son of Joseph?" or if he groups "Is not this—Jesus the son of Joseph?" The way the reader groups these words will tell his listeners whether we are concerned with one of several men named Jesus or with one man named Jesus who is the son of Joseph.

2. The reader must give attention to the relationship of the word groups. There is, of course, the relationship of a principal and subordinate clause. There are also such relationships as cause-effect and the parallelisms which occur frequently in Old Testament literature.

---

[5] Wayne N. Thompson and Seth A. Fessenden, *Basic Experiences in Speech* (Englewood Cliffs, N. J.: Prentice-Hall, Inc., 1958), p. 86.

Parrish stresses the importance of these relationships in communicating the meaning of a selection:

> The constituent units of a sentence are seldom merely strung together like beads; they are of different sizes and purposes, like the girders of a steel bridge, and bear various relationships to each other. These relationships are an integral part of meaning.[6]

By taking care in grouping words and in determining the proper relationship of word groups, the reader can more ably use pauses and duration to communicate the selection's meaning. Everett Parker points up the importance of grouping as well as the possible differences between written and oral punctuation. He identifies the method as *phrasing* rather than grouping.

> One of the most common faults in speech is rate of utterance. Sentences phrases, and even single words are spoken without linking them together in a conscious thought pattern. Or the speaker falls into a speech tune that repeats itself over and over without regard to the interpretative demands of the script content. What actually happens is that the speaker himself comes to understand the meaning of what he is saying only after he has spoken the words. The audience, of course, may not get the meaning at all. . . . Phrase your content carefully according to the thought pattern. . . . Phrasing is determined by weighing the relative values of the various word groups in terms of the total idea. It does not necessarily follow the punctuation used in writing. Punctuation is for the eye, phrasing for the ear.[7]

Another equally important aid is the method of centering. The reader attempts to direct the attention of his hearers to or focus their attention on key words and phrases while moving easily and perhaps rapidly over those portions deemed to be less important. Albright provides us with a succinct and clear description of this method:

> If the mind centers on important idea-carrying words and phrases, and relegates the others into the background of attention, expression is improved and heightened. Prominence is usually given (1) to new ideas at the expense of those that may have been mentioned before; (2) to ideas that show change or contrast in relation to others; and, in

[6] W. M. Parrish, *Reading Aloud* (New York: The Ronald Press Company, 1953), p. 30.

[7] Everett C. Parker, *Religious Television: What to Do and How* (New York: Harper & Row, Publishers, 1961), p. 163.

general, (3) to main ideas as opposed to parenthetical or subordinate ones.[8]

RHYTHM

Rhythm is the means by which the several aspects of time can be combined into a unified expression or interpretation. Whether the selection contains the irregular, changing rhythms of prose or the more regular, metered rhythms of poetry, its rhythm must be discovered and appreciated if the various time factors are to fall into place and contribute to a total impression. An important clue to the rhythm is the mood, for emotion both causes rhythm and is produced by rhythm. If the reader can catch the rhythm which moved the author as he wrote, he may then enter naturally into the movement of the selection.

Most readers could improve their use of rhythm if they would focus on artistic purpose, appreciation of the selection, and abandon in expression. When the reader genuinely feels that the use of a particular rhythm will heighten his communication of the mood and meaning, he has taken the first step in learning to use rhythm. In this perspective, rhythm will support and reinforce meaning and mood, not supplant them. The sense of fulfilling one's artistic purpose through the use of rhythm carries one beyond mechanical execution of meter and stress to a fuller and freer communication through rhythm. When the reader's experience reaches this point, then the communication of rhythm is not a trial but an enjoyable endeavor.

Now let us turn to two kinds of appreciation which will help the reader develop a greater ability to communicate through rhythm. The first comes from the development of an "auditory imagination." We are indebted to T. S. Eliot for his development and description of this concept.

> What I call the "auditory imagination" is the feeling for syllable and rhythm, penetrating far below the conscious levels of thought and feeling, invigorating every word; sinking to the most primitive and forgotten, returning to the origin and bringing something back, seeking the beginning and the end. It works through meanings, certainly, or not without meanings in the ordinary sense, and fuses the old and obliter-

[8] H. D. Albright, *Working Up a Part* (Boston: Houghton Mifflin Company, 1947), p. 43.

> ated and the trite, the current, and the new and surprising, the most ancient and the most civilized mentality.[9]

Every reader should endeavor to cultivate his auditory imagination so that he has a feeling for syllable and rhythm. As he reads, a host of clues suggesting how the selection might sound as it is read aloud should stir his imagination.

When reading poetry the reader may quicken his appreciation of the rhythm of a poem by following Carl Burklund's advice and viewing the poem as symphonic structure:

> A poem is one large rhythm, which is its unity, its vital form, is composed of the confluence or fusion of a number of lesser rhythms which condition, support and enhance the power of one another. . . . A poem is a symphonic structure, an organic rhythm, composed of the living interaction of a number of lesser rhythms which are divisible into those related to meaning and those related to music.[10]

If a poem is viewed as Burklund suggests, then the rhythm is more than counting out the meter and plotting the stress—it is understood and appreciated as an integral and basic ingredient of the poem. Rhythm is not something imposed on meaning and structure; it is in the heart of the theme and mood and expresses itself in and through the words and structure. The reader, then, comes to appreciate the rhythm by approaching through the heart—the core—of the poem and following it out into words and grammatical structure.

Finally, the reader should attempt to express rhythm with abandon. Few cautious or conservative readers will ever experience the aesthetic pleasure which rhythm gives, and consequently their use of rhythm will seem wooden and perhaps mechanical. The majority of readers will need to push themselves into an abandon in the expression of rhythm which they will deem to be "overdone." Most readers need to be more adventuresome rather than more restrained when it comes to communicating rhythm.

As a concluding caution to those few readers who might carry this suggestion of abandon to the extreme, let us consider again the words of Walter Dill Scott.

---

[9] T. S. Eliot, *The Use of Poetry and the Use of Criticism* (Cambridge, Massachusetts: Harvard University Press, 1933), p. 111.

[10] Carl E. Burklund, "Poetry: A Symphonic Structure," *The Quarterly Journal of Speech*, XXXVII, No. 2 (1951), pp. 182-83.

It is aesthetically displeasing to have too much made of rhythm in reading prose and poetry, but the highest manifestations of art are present when the rhythmical form is used to express the thought. We do not like to have that which is most important subordinated to the least important, but our aesthetic natures crave rhythm, and when the best expression of thought coincides with the production of rhythm, we respond at once with enthusiastic approval.[11]

[11] Walter Dill Scott, *The Psychology of Public Speaking* (Philadelphia: Pearson Brothers, 1907), pp. 145-46.

Chapter 10

The Reading Text and Its Use

Unless your handwriting or printing is unusually legible, do not read from such copy and, except in emergencies, do not read from the handwriting of other persons. Books and magazines are suitable only if the print is sufficiently large and distinct, if adequate space occurs between the lines, and if ample margins exist.

EUGENE E. WHITE*

The copy from which one reads and the way he uses that copy should contribute to his oral reading. Most readers will be inclined to say "granted" and then wish to go on to some more interesting topic. However, the fact remains that, in many oral readings, either the copy used or the way it is used does detract from the reading. This unfortunate effect occurs because readers regard the copy and its use as a minor matter; consequently they devote too little time to preparation of the copy and practice in its use. This chapter will indicate the contribution which good copy and able use of it make to oral reading. In addition, specific suggestions will be given for the selection, preparation, and use of the reading copy.

When a reader is working from poor copy or when he is not adept in utilizing this copy, his reading is affected in many ways. Easily observed are the loss of eye contact, limitation of communicative bodily action,

* *Practical Speech Fundamentals* (New York: The Macmillan Company, 1960), p. 401.

and poor vocal quality and projection. Damaging as these effects are to communicative reading, they are only symptoms of a far more serious injury to the interpretative act.

In addition to the difficulties just mentioned, the reader has less time and less attention to devote to the personal appreciation of his reading. He experiences less impression and is capable of less expression. Moreover, his relationship with his audience is affected. Conscious that he is less direct and that he is less capable of communicating the full meaning and mood of his selection, the reader becomes more aware of his audience as critics applying certain standards of judgment to his performance. Likewise, his relationship to the literary piece is changed. Now he thinks less of it as something to be enjoyed than as something to be properly grouped and pronounced. Finally, his relationship to the act of reading aloud is affected. He relinquishes the concept of sharing that which has become meaningful and moving to him and embraces the aim of accurately conveying what is on the printed page.

Thus, although the preparation and use of the reading copy may be regarded as minor matters, every reader needs to bear in mind that they have major consequences. Their neglect will adversely affect almost all aspects of the oral presentation of his reading. Conversely, proper preparation and use of the reading copy will enhance eye contact, communicative bodily action, timing, and vocal quality and projection. It will give the reader more opportunity to personally appreciate his material as he reads it aloud. Moreover, it will improve his relationship to his material, to his audience, and to the act of oral interpretation. No reader can afford to neglect such a wide opportunity for improvement.

GENERAL TEXTUAL PREPARATION

Frequently the reader has the opportunity to select the kind of copy from which he will read. If there are several books in which your selection may be found, you can consider which one would be the most easily readable. Or, if the minister is purchasing a Bible, book of prayers, or copy of the liturgy, he has the opportunity to consider which publication is best for use in oral reading. If your material will be copied by typewriter, then you can make suggestions about the kind of paper used, spacing, breaking lines, and so forth.

What merits should the reader seek in copy from which he intends to read aloud? When dealing with the subject of manuscript preaching in

1849, Henry J. Ripley gave some specific advice about the manuscript itself:

> A discourse, intended to be . . . preached, should be written on paper of the quarto form, so that large quantities of matter may be under the eye at once, and as infrequent occasion as possible exist for turning over the leaves. The writing should also be of such size as to be distinctly legible without the preacher's stooping, or making any special effort. The paragraphs ought to be very distinct from each other, and the emphatic words underscored. The lower corner of each leaf should be partially bent up so that the leaf may be instantly turned without a failure, and without the accident of turning more leaves than one at a time.[1]

We can draw several criteria for readable texts from Ripley's remarks.

1. The material should be easy to read. This means a clear type of good size, well spaced, with a sharp contrast between page and print. The policy of dividing words at the ends of lines and pages, as well as the carrying of a sentence from one page to another, should be examined to make certain that the reader will not find it confusing.

2. Important divisions should be clearly indicated by spacing, indentation, and perhaps titles and subtitles. If one has been used to reading from a Bible that has each verse distinctly set apart, and then attempts to read from a Bible where several verses are grouped together without such distinct markings, he may have considerable difficulty with his public reading until he has adjusted to the different format.

It will be helpful for the reader to know if he is viewing one prayer with several paragraphs or if each paragraph is a separate prayer. Breaks in printing of the liturgy accompanied by instructions for appropriate action and attitude are likewise valuable to the reader. Some preachers who desire to use a manuscript find their material easier to read when they employ some of the methods used by Peter Marshall to indicate groupings or a climactic or anticlimactic sequence of words or phrases:

It is not easy to live out your life day after day
and week after week
and year after year in a subordinate
position while somebody else gets the notice
the publicity

[1] Henry J. Ripley, *Sacred Rhetoric* (Boston: Gould, Kendall, & Lincoln, 1849), p. 165.

the attention
the credit
the praise
the spotlight
and perhaps the reward.[2]

Frequently Marshall would set a single sentence apart with the same spacing and indentation given to paragraphs. Most oral readers will prefer material that is well spaced, appropriately indented, and accurately titled, as opposed to crowded, undivided, and unidentified material.

3. Where there are several pages to be read, the pages should allow rapid and accurate movement. Some pocket rituals and pocket Bibles are printed on very thin paper. Frequently their pages simply defy rapid separation and turning. Other types of paper seem slick, and pages printed on such paper can be slippery and hard to turn. Occasionally the way the book is bound or the pages fastened together impedes manipulation of the pages.

In setting forth suggestions for a radio script, Waldo Abbot provides us with criteria for a typed manuscript.

> The manscript should be double spaced in order to allow for easy reading. It should be clean so that it will be easy to follow. Be sure that the pages are arranged correctly. . . . Do not clip the sheets together. Use a type of paper that does not easily rattle. Onion skin is perhaps the worst. Typewriter bond paper is decidedly noisy. The pulp copy paper used in newspaper offices is probably the best.[3]

A special consideration for pastors is the copy used for services where changes must be made in the ritual from singular to plural and from masculine to feminine. This is true in the ritual for baptism and for the burial of the dead where the singular and the masculine are printed. Frequently they are in a different type to indicate that they may be altered if needed. In the case of the baptismal ritual inexpensive copies can be purchased and proper number and gender written in the blanks provided in the copy. Inexpensive copies of the wedding service can also be purchased and the names of the bride and groom

---

[2] Peter Marshall, *Mr. Jones, Meet the Master* (Westwood, N. J.: Fleming H. Revell Co., 1949), p. 53.

[3] Waldo Abbot, *Handbook of Broadcasting* (New York: McGraw-Hill Book Company, Inc., 1941), p. 30.

written in the appropriate blanks. Such a practice simplifies the reading task, for the pastor does not have to recall the correct number, gender, or name as the ritual may require.

PREPARATION FOR THE SERVICE

Once you have selected the text or copy from which you will read, your next task will be to prepare that copy for reading. The reader should go through his copy carefully and thoroughly to be certain that all pages are present and in order, that all the copy is clearly readable, and that there are no errors in the copy. If any of these problems are encountered, the copy should be corrected neatly or new copy secured.

If there is more than one unit of copy, the units should be organized and the material clearly identified. Frequently, in leading a service of worship, several different things will be read aloud. Such items as *calls to worship* and *collects* may appear in the morning bulletin. Other parts of the service may be read from a section in a hymnal, a book of ritual, or a book of prayers. In addition, the scripture lesson is read from the Bible, whereas the sermon may be read from a manuscript, or quotations included in the sermon may be read from other books or pamphlets. On occasion, an episcopal letter may be read; there may also be announcements which must be read aloud. If the church has a divided chancel there will be the added problem of having the appropriate materials at the lectern and at the pulpit. In some instances different materials may be needed at the altar and at the baptismal font or at the chancel rail.

If the worship leader wishes to avoid awkward breaks in the movement of the worship service, he needs to have the materials in their proper order and place; the point at which he is to start reading should be clearly marked. Within the ritual of a given church the leader may have alternate orders, as well as several options within a specific order of worship. In such instances there is a real need to clearly designate the portions which he intends to read.

The reader should consider whether the size and number of items will be manageable in the reading situation. Is there ample room on the altar, pulpit, lectern, reader's stand, or table to accommodate the texts? Is there a space where completed items may be placed? The angle or pitch of the top of the reader's stand or lectern may also be important. The reader may find that his various reading copies are inclined to slide off the lectern.

Such details may be considered trivial, but failure to plan for these trivial details frequently results in an otherwise able and well-prepared interpreter doing an inadequate job of presenting a reading. Not only do they affect the reader at particular points in his presentation, but they are sufficiently distracting to prevent him from reaching his normal interpretive effectiveness. Moreover, the appreciation of the audience is affected because their attention is attracted by the difficulties the reader experiences in locating and handling his material.

When preparing copy to be read, the reader should develop good methods of preparation and then be consistent in their use. Once he becomes familiar with certain methods and skillful in their use, he will have a better opportunity to discover which methods need improving.

PRACTICE READING OF THE PREPARED COPY

Having selected good copy, organized it, marked it clearly, and adapted it to the reading situation is only a good beginning. The reader needs to go over the copy several times so that he is completely familiar with it and experienced in using it. One should not prepare to read the scripture lesson by reading aloud from a personal copy of the Bible, and then for his public reading "sight read" the pulpit Bible. If he intends to read from the pulpit Bible, he should go to the sanctuary and practice reading from it.

USE OF THE READING COPY

Read the liturgy, Bible, prayer books, and other aids to worship aloud. Do not memorize the material in order to present it from memory rather than read it aloud. Do not attempt to paraphrase the liturgy in order to achieve the merits of extemporaneous delivery. The portions of the worship service which we interpret orally free us from the task of recall and impromptu composition so that we can enter more fully into the meaning of these parts of the service. Moreover, they allow us to supplement our personal leadership with the rich heritage of the faith. As Parsons and Jones state:

> Whatever its deficiencies, the Prayer Book is a repository of the best of the past. It represents not the passing mood of the moment, but the durable experience of the church of the ages. . . . It releases the congregation from the affliction of individual idiosyncrasy. It affords prayers for all kinds of persons, and for all the manifold issues of life, because it has grown from the common experience of all. It is balanced, stable, conveying by its very form the changeless strength of God.[4]

Thus the first suggestion is that we actually read from our prepared copy when interpreting orally.

The reader should also be aware of the symbolism of the physical presence of the copy or text from which he is reading. For one thing, it signifies to the listener that this is not a paraphrase or commentary but that the leader is reading the actual words. In the case of the Bible and of the designated liturgy of a church, the text signifies that it is the Word of God being read or that it is a historic rite and ceremony of the church in which we are now participating. Again, the book or paper held in the reader's hand may suggest to his hearers that this matter is so important that the reader wishes us to have the verbatim statement, as in the case of a reference to the law of the church. Thus the text or copy from which one reads may be used as a sign.

Then, too, the reading copy can be used as a part of the reader's gestures. If the text is small enough to be held in one hand, the reader should gesture freely as if he were not holding his reading copy. He should not allow the book from which he is reading to immobilize the hand and arm which support it. You may recall seeing Billy Graham gesture with his Bible as he reads from it during one of his crusades.

SUMMARY

In conclusion, remember that the copy from which you read aloud and the way you use that copy should contribute to your oral reading rather than detract from it. To achieve this end you should select clear, properly spaced, clean copy which can be easily handled. When preparing the copy for reading, see that it is in proper reading order, with selections clearly marked, and that it is suitable to the conditions of

---

[4] Edward Lambe Parsons and Bayard Hale Jones, *The American Prayer Book* (New York: Charles Scribner's Sons, 1937), pp. 9-10.

the reading situation. Use this copy for your practice reading so that you will be familiar with it. When reading aloud, appreciate the potential of the text in terms of sign and gesture and use it for these purposes where appropriate.

PART THREE: ORAL INTERPRETATION OF THE WORSHIP SERVICE

Chapter II

Oral Interpretation of the Formal Service of Worship

All religious experience shows this inevitable drawing out of the soul toward the "wholly other," which takes the form of reverence and of longing for communion and fellowship. In its primary sense, therefore, worship is just this reverent approach to God, and consciousness of the values that reside in him. It is, as Edgar S. Brightman calls it, a matter of the inner posture of the individual.

WARREN N. NEVIUS*

There are several ways in which better oral interpretation can improve the leadership of the Sunday morning worship service. Good oral reading can accentuate the unity of the whole service. For many religious leaders the worship service has become fragmented. They lead it a unit at a time, without an adequate awareness of the pattern of the service or the relation of one unit to another. As a worship service ought to move meaningfully and in unity, let us consider

* *Religion as Experience and Truth* (Philadelphia: The Westminster Press, 1941), p. 101.

several means by which the leader may give more unity to the worship service.

The leader can emphasize the unity of the service for himself during his preparation. As he selects and composes the various items in the service, he can locate them in the over-all pattern (adoration, confession, affirmation, and dedication) and consider their contribution to that particular phase of the service. The leader can also go through the entire service each time he practices it orally. This sort of rehearsal of the leadership tasks will emphasize the total pattern of the service.

Those sentences or phrases used to lead the congregation into the next act of worship (verbal rubrics) are very important to the preservation of the unity of the service. They are like the couplings that join the cars of a train. They must firmly lock the units of the service together. Sentences such as *The Lord be with you, Let us pray, Let us worship God with our tithes and offerings,* and *Let us hear the word of God* serve to link the units of the service together.

Once, after working with a pastor on several parts of the worship service—the call to worship, the prayers, the Scriptures, the responsive reading, and the sermon—I went to hear him conduct the service in his own sanctuary. The contrast between the units we had worked on and the sentences mentioned above was appalling. The Scripture was read well and we were moved by it; then in an inaudible, indifferent monotone, the preacher rattled off *Let us pray* and we were thrown back to our former apathy. So the service went, surging forward and then sliding backward. The next time we met, we labored hard on those vital links in the service.

There are many ways in which worship leaders can strengthen their leadership when using these key sentences. One valuable aid is the use of emphasis. Most of the time the leader makes no attempt to vary the force of his voice while reading these sentences. In the sentence *Let us pray,* emphasis makes an important difference. An army chaplain leading worship with a congregation of soldiers in a staging area or a replacement depot might well want to place the emphasis on the first word—"*Let* us pray." In placing emphasis on the word *let* he could urge everyone present to join in the act of prayer. On the other hand, a pastor calling a congregation that shared a common problem might wish to emphasize the word *us*—"Let *us* pray." Still another pastor, who sensed that his people might easily enter into the act of prayer while still preoccupied with the concerns of the day, might want to emphasize the word *pray*—"Let us *pray*." By placing the emphasis on *pray* he might suggest that we should pray rather than do something else, or that we should truly or really pray. Thus the use of emphasis can give these guiding sentences added meaning for the particular congregation.

Another means of improving these sentences is to vary pitch or to employ a better melody pattern. Frequently these sentences are read in a monotone, or else a wrong melody pattern is employed. Considering the same sentence, a frequent error (as indicated in an earlier chapter) is an extreme rise in pitch on the last word so that we feel a question is being asked.

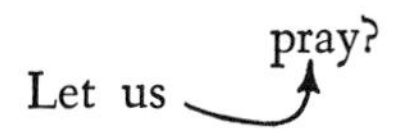

This is the same pitch as a reader might use for the word *away* when asking the question, "Are you going *away?*"

It may be that those who are accustomed to formulating the sentence as an interrogative do not see a problem in this pitch pattern. For such persons let us simply say that verbal directives should not be put in the interrogative form. One pastor learned this lesson the hard way. In response to his *Shall we pray?*, a boyish voice vigorously and emphatically replied, *No!* Much amused by this unexpected response, the congregation found serious participation in the ensuing prayer difficult. Equally unfortunate is the pattern of declining pitch and force which suggests that the leader is weary or bored with the service.

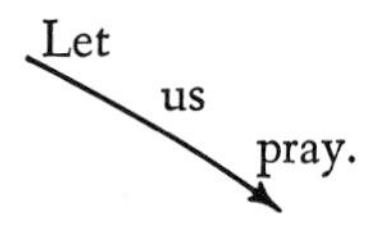

This is similar to the melody and force which a person might use when saying with resignation, "Let's get it over with."

Rather than giving the wrong meaning, some leaders seem to give no meaning to these sentences, for the words are spoken at the same pitch level and with the same force. Such a reading sounds mechanical, as though the leader were simply going through an oft-repeated routine.

A limited and paced lowering of pitch might suggest the seriousness of this act of worship.

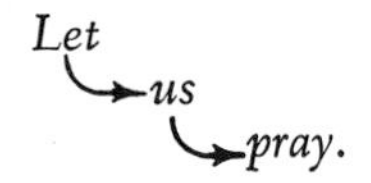

A controlled and paced rise in pitch might suggest the anticipation of communion with God.

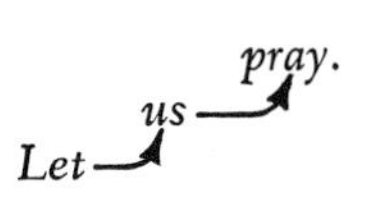

These are purposeful, controlled steps in pitch intended to communicate a particular meaning.

A third factor in improving the delivery of these sentences is the reader's rate of utterance. Frequently the errors of monotony in pitch and force are compounded by monotony in rate as well. It is not uncommon to hear the words in these sentences rapidly rattled off in a manner similar to Winchell's "Mister and Mrs. America and all the ships at sea, let's go to press." This error is most pronounced when the leader is conscious of a crowded service which is apt to exceed the customary time of dismissal. Not only does such a mechanical rapidity of rate ruin the mood and rob the service of meaning, it also leads to faulty articulation. We are apt to hear *Let us spray* instead of *Let us pray,* or we may even hear *Let us bray*. A more deliberate reading of that sentence with a brief pause before the word *pray* makes it possible for the reader to avoid this mistake. An equally unfortunate error is the eliding of the first two words so that the worshiper is reminded of the supermarket rather than the sanctuary. He hears *lettuce pray* rather than *Let us pray*. Again, a deliberate rate with a very brief pause after *let* is a reliable remedy.

In addition, the leader should make certain that the strength or force of voice used in the reading of these verbal rubrics is comparable to the voice he uses to read the rest of the service. As indicated earlier, some leaders actually become inaudible when reading these sentences. Others use such a weak voice that they sound timid when calling us to participate in the acts of worship. There ought to be relatively uniform audibility to suggest the unity of the service.

The unity of the worship service can be strengthened by the utilization of emphasis, pitch, and rate so as to read these directive, transitional sentences with meaning and feeling. When they are so read, the sentences will command the attention of the entire congregation, guide the worshipers accurately through the various stages of worship, and help them participate more fully in the worship service.

Occasionally the difficulty arises not so much from a lack of understanding of the significance of the leadership tasks or from an inability to read aloud, but rather from an unfortunate view of ourselves and of our role as worship leaders. Professor Nevius warns us about this danger. "The weakness of the priesthood lies . . . in the tendency of its members to conceive of themselves as a class apart and the sole custodians of religious truth and thus to regard the priestly functions as ends and not as means." [1] Difficulty in oral interpretation of the verbal rubrics may mean that the leader should examine his concept of the role of the leader of worship.

The leader should strive for uniform quality of preparation and presentation for the entire service. When each part of the service makes its full contribution to the whole, every part of the service is strengthened. The sermon, for example, is significantly strengthened when it is presented in the context of a worship service which is properly arranged and well conducted.

Many worship leaders unknowingly destroy the unity of the worship service by neglecting various parts of the service and concentrating ninety per cent or more of their preparation on two or three items such as the sermon, the pastoral prayer, and the Scripture. When they read the call to worship, offertory sentences, responsive reading, and like items, they sound as though they are on unfamiliar and unimportant ground. Not only does the service alternate back and forth between seemingly important and unimportant acts, but it may well be that one phase or step such as *adoration* is so weak as to fail to help the worshiper—consequently it is difficult, to secure either a contrite confession or an enthusiastic affirmation of faith.

During his period of preparation and oral practice, the reader should give specific attention to each part of the worship service for which he has leadership responsibility, including the benediction. By reading each unit well, he will make clear its meaning for the service and its particular contribution to the whole. He will further assist the congregation to participate in and benefit from the various acts. As Dr. Harkness explains:

> Corporate worship . . . is conducted by a leader and proceeds through regular forms. . . . It can be a great aid to worship, for tested forms and the direction given by a person whose vocation it is to conduct public worship can go far toward eliminating trial and error. Many who

---

[1] Warren Nelson Nevius, *Religion as Experience and Truth* (Philadelphia: The Westminster Press, 1941), p. 100.

> are baffled at the idea of conducting their own private devotions are able to worship helpfully under guidance at church.[2]

Another way of developing a more meaningful and unified service is for the leader himself to be a worshiper, and to worship as he is leading the service. In this way he experiences the unity and progression of the worship acts. He leads by example as well as by precept. Because he is spiritually benefiting from the unity of the worship service, he can communicate that unity with a fuller appreciation of its meaning and significance.

In order to both experience and communicate the unity of the worship service which they are leading, most leaders will have to deal with two problems. The first is the inability of leaders to consistently enter into each leadership responsibility as a worshiper. Some men find the formality and the responsibility for leading the congregation so distracting that they have persistent difficulties in attempting to participate in the service as a worshiper. Others find themselves behaving like a swimmer who swims with his head under water for a few strokes, then comes up for air, then ducks back under water to swim a few more strokes and again comes up for air. They worship and lead for a while, then they stop worshiping and only lead the service so that they may observe how everything in the service is functioning. Later they go back to worshiping and leading, and so it goes throughout the remainder of the service.

This vacillation in the leader's own inner posture as a worshiper impairs his immediate awareness of the unifying factors in the service and the manner in which the service is progressing. At key points, because he is not himself worshiping, his soul is not meeting the Most High and consequently he cannot make answer with his mind, heart, and will. Because he is not in the vanguard of worshipers approaching the throne of grace, he is not able to fully express the movement toward God. As one author put it, he is like the spoon that is used to carry the soup to the mouth. He conveys the nourishment but does not partake of it.

Many leaders find it helpful to establish new priorities for their leadership activity. They make their own total involvement in worship the matter of first importance. Then they rank other qualities, such as vocal adequacy, awareness of congregational response, appropriateness,

---

[2] Georgia Harkness, *Prayer and the Common Life* (New York: Abingdon Press, 1948), p. 154.

adherence to dismissal time, and so forth, in their proper order. They make their response in worship central and the other matters peripheral. Proceeding on the conviction that their personal response in worship is the thing most needed, they are able to perform their leadership tasks more ably.

A second difficulty in leading worship accrues from the rarity of the capacity for religious emotion. T. S. Eliot poses this problem in a discussion of religious poetry:

> The capacity for writing poetry is rare, the capacity for religious emotion of the first intensity is rare; and it is to be expected that the existence of both capacities in the same individual should be rarer still. People who write devotional verse are usually writing as they want to feel, rather than as they do feel.[3]

It might also be said that most worship leaders are attempting to lead their congregations into a worship experience that they themselves want to feel rather than into an experience that they do feel.

Participation in spiritual retreats, ashrams, and other activities which increase the capacity for religious emotion is helpful in meeting this problem. Immediately prior to leading services of worship, reading of devotional literature intended to evoke those feelings which accompany adoration, confession, affirmation, and dedication may also serve to stimulate our capacity for religious feeling. A reminder placed on the desk or lectern might encourage further effort to enlarge our capacity for religious emotion. This warning from Robert Burns may prove useful for such a purpose:

> Compared with this, how poor Religion's pride,
> In all the pomp of method and of art,
> Where men display to congregation's wide,
> Devotion's ev'ry grace, except the heart![4]

If the leader fails to worship as he leads the service, then a prayer of pardon may be prayed as though it pertained only to the people and not to himself. Or, the call to pray the Lord's prayer may be voiced in a cold and official manner. The leader must feel his own need for prayer

---

[3] T. S. Eliot, *After Strange Gods* (London: Faber & Faber, Ltd., 1934), p. 29.

[4] Allen Cunningham, *The Poetical Works of Robert Burns* (Philadelphia: Porter & Coates, 1882), p. 159.

—a need made more urgent by an immediate awareness of God's presence.

Finally, the leader who keeps before him the tremendous goal toward which he leads the people will be aided in his endeavor to communicate the meaning and the movement of the service. Wesley urges us to remember that the whole value of congregational prayer, hearing the Scriptures read, and receiving the Lord's Supper depends on their actual conducing to the knowledge and love of God.[5]

Professor Hugh Blair uttered similar sentiments in his lectures at the University of Edinburgh:

> Never let the capital principle with which we set out at first, be forgotten—to keep close in view the great end for which a preacher mounts a pulpit; even to infuse good dispositions into his hearers, to persuade them to serve God, and to become better men.[6]

Keeping the end for which he leads people in worship constantly before him will help the leader sense how all parts of the service are functioning in unison to move the congregation to a fuller knowledge and love of God.

SUMMARY

Subsequent chapters will discuss in detail the public reading of prayers, the Scriptures, responsive reading, and hymns. In this chapter we have considered the following general principles for improving the oral reading of the worship service:

1. Emphasize the unity of the worship service during your preparation for conducting it.
2. Read the verbal rubrics or worship directives well.
3. Strive for uniform quality of preparation and presentation.
4. Worship as you attempt to lead the service of worship.
5. Keep the high goal of congregational worship before you as you lead the service.

---

[5] E. H. Sugden, *The Standard Sermons of John Wesley* (London: The Epworth Press, 1935), pp. 242-43.

[6] Hugh Blair, *Lectures on Rhetoric and Belles Lettres* (London: Charles Daly, 1838), p. 393.

Let every religious leader keep the spiritual hunger of the people he leads in his mind and heart. T. S. Eliot has put the matter well: "The number of half-alive hungry for any form of spiritual experience, or what offers itself as spiritual experience, high or low, good or bad, is considerable. My own generation has not served them very well." [7] Remembering Eliot's remarks, let us strive to serve our people well through more meaningful and moving oral interpretation of the worship service.

---

[7] Eliot, *After Strange Gods,* p. 61.

Chapter 12

Oral Interpretation of Prayers

Leading a congregation in public prayer is a work of art demanding expert skill and painstaking preparation. . . . In nonliturgical churches the minister does not kneel in the chancel, facing the altar, as though addressing himself to the Most High. He stands in the pulpit, facing the congregation. That obvious fact defines his function in public prayer. He is trying so to phrase the soul's adoration, thanksgiving, penitence, petitions and intercessions, that the people may be caught up into his prayer and may themselves pray with him. That is a sacred soul-searching task. It calls for deep and sympathetic insight into human need, for sensitive awareness of both individual and social problems, and for faith in God's grace and mercy; and it demands dedicated and careful preparation as much as does the preaching of a sermon.

HARRY EMERSON FOSDICK*

Every worship leader who desires to interpret prayers well orally has to find answers to three questions: "How can I pray myself when I am leading the congregation in prayer? What is leadership in prayer? How can I pray with and for people rather than at or against them?"

* *A Book of Public Prayers* (New York: Harper & Row, Publishers, 1959), pp. 7-8.

PERSONAL PARTICIPATION IN PRAYER

The religious leader finds it difficult to pray as spontaneously and genuinely in public as he does in his private devotions or in pastoral calls, because public leadership in prayer involves several new factors. One example is voice. Public leadership in prayer requires a vocal projection of sufficient strength to enable the worshiper to hear the leader easily.

In his personal prayer life and when praying with a parishoner or a family group, the leader probably uses a voice that is somewhat quieter or softer than the voice he uses in regular conversation. Now, however, the leader has to do the opposite. He must use a voice that is much louder than his conversational voice. This required change in vocal behavior causes many leaders to lose the feeling of prayer. They feel like they are preaching rather than praying.

Leaders need to develop more responsiveness and abandon in the voice they use for reading prayers in worship services. It may prove helpful for the leader to first read the prayer as a part of his own private devotions. Then let him attempt to read the prayer in the voice required for audibility in the sanctuary, capturing the mood and genuineness which he experienced as he prayed privately. Another way of experiencing more vocal freedom in reading prayers is to consciously attempt to step up your projection in mood so that it is comparable to the increase in projection of voice. You want not just more force, but more intensity of vocal quality as well. In this regard the reader might improve his projection of mood by reading aloud daily from the Book of Psalms, making a special effort to express such moods as adoration, confession, thanksgiving, and dedication.

A second difference between the situations of public prayer and private prayer is the degree of complexity. Public worship requires that the prayer fit into the total worship service. The larger congregation necessitates a prayer which will meet many and varied needs, and leadership which adjusts to varying responses. If other persons are sharing the leadership responsibilities, there is a need to cooperate with them to provide a coherent and unified leadership. The more complex the worship activity, the greater the number of potential distractions which may confront the leader. This means that a more intense concentration is required when attempting to lead a public service.

Thoughts about other participants or other parts of the worship service must be rigidly evicted, and the leader must intensify his efforts to participate fully in the prayer.

Dean Charles Reynolds Brown assures us that even in the midst of conducting the worship service such a thing is possible. "The minister standing in the midst of a great congregation may nevertheless by the concentration of mind and soul, by his utter absorption in the high task in which he is engaged, enter into his closet and close the door." [1]

Another factor which is prominent in public prayer is the formality of the service. Some leaders seem frozen by this formality. They become more concerned with dignity and decorum than with the Deity. Such formality may appear in a studied pattern of emphasis and rise and fall in pitch. It may take the form of overenunciation or affected pronunciation. Because this curse of formalism is no respecter of denomination or personal achievement, every leader needs to fight against it. The most promising remedy for formality is to set a higher goal for your leadership and strenuously strive to achieve it. Let the leader's goal be pastoral. Let him strive to catch his people up in his prayer and to help them pray with him. Henry Ward Beecher's testimony suggests how prayer with such a goal soars beyond mere formality:

> Hundreds of times as I rose to pray and glanced at the congregation, I could not keep back the tears. There came to my mind such a sense of their wants, there were so many hidden sorrows, so many weights and burdens, so many doubts and dangers, so many states of weakness! I had such a sense of compassion for them, that it seemed to me as if I could hardly open my mouth to speak. When I take my people and carry them before God to plead for them . . . there is no time that Jesus is so crowned with glory, no time when I get so far into heaven as then. I forget the body, I live in the spirit. It seems as if God permitted me to lay my hand on the very Tree of Life and shake down from it both leaves and fruit for the healing of my people.[2]

A fourth difference between private and public prayer is the matter of timing. In private prayer we can proceed according to the pace of our own participation. Pacing the prayer in a pastoral call requires only that we adjust to the responsiveness of a single parishoner or a small group of parishoners. However, the problem of meaningful timing in public prayer is greatly amplified because of the large number of

[1] Charles Reynolds Brown, *The Art of Preaching* (New York: The Macmillan Company, 1922), p. 215.

[2] *Ibid.*, p. 216.

worshipers and the consequent range of their inclinations and ability to participate in prayer. Difficult as the problem is, it must be solved because of the lyrical nature of prayer, which requires rhythmical expression. In addition, there is the need to coordinate the rhythm essential to the communication of meaning with the rhythm of receipt of the leader's guidance and the response to it. The latter requirement is the one which leaders of worship most frequently violate.

The key to a proper coordination of the rhythm of your prayer leadership with the rhythm of the congregation's response is found in a keen and lively empathy with the congregation. Bishop McConnell describes the degree of empathy required:

> Leading in prayer means uttering the petition which the people would utter if they could. The people are refreshed if the preacher prays in such terms that they can heartily say *Amen,* if they seem to hear themselves praying in speech they would use if they could, speech that is not theirs by their own utterance but theirs by immediate sanction as soon as they hear it. . . . The masters in any field, we repeat, are those who have caught the spirit of their time and have so uttered it that it becomes a genuine voice of humanity.[3]

At the very least, the rate of your leadership in prayer cannot be primarily determined by discovering the rate that best suits your own taste or your ability to read aloud. A rate that best communicates the meaning of the prayer and a rate that is most helpful for congregational participation must be prior criteria.

The worship leader can facilitate his personal participation in the prayers he reads aloud by developing more vocal responsiveness and abandon, a higher concentration of mind and soul, a pastoral goal for his leadership in prayer, and a rate and rhythm of prayer which allow a maximum communication of meaning and empathy with the congregation.

LEADERSHIP IN PRAYER

Now let us consider the second question raised at the outset of this chapter: "What is leadership in prayer?" Leadership in prayer is, first of all, example. When the leader enters the chancel, pauses before the

[3] Francis John McConnell, *The Preacher and the People* (New York: Abingdon Press, 1922), pp. 107-8.

altar, and bows in silent prayer or takes his seat by the pulpit or lectern and bows in silent prayer, he is leading by example. When the leader pauses before he starts to pray, concentrates on what he is about to do, enters into the mood of prayer, and then begins to read the prayer aloud, he is leading through example. Particularly when the leader personally participates in the prayer, entering fully into the stages of adoration, confession, thanksgiving, and dedication, does he lead by example. The matter of leadership by example can be summed up by simply saying that to lead prayer one needs to be in prayer.

In addition to personal example, the leader also gives guidance to the congregation. He calls the congregation to prayer and indicates when the prayer is concluded. He may also designate the nature of the prayer, such as confession or dedication. If the prayer follows a particular pattern, using such means as emphasis and mood, he will guide the congregation through the pattern. In bidding prayers or in a litany such guidance may be explicit, whereas in invocations, prayers of confession, and pastoral prayers the explicit directives may be very brief or even omitted and reliance placed on implicit suggestions.

To guide people through the prayers of a worship service the leader must be thoroughly familiar with the congregation and the sort of leadership which they need. In addition, he must be skilled in leadership so that he can lead prayer with both ease and pleasure. The person who dislikes public prayer or finds it difficult to lead will discover that his own attitudes cause him to stumble as he endeavors to lead others.

Not only example and guidance but also a sharing of his own prayer experience is required of the leader of public prayer. Leadership in prayer requires an openness of soul. We must be willing to share—to expose our soul's realization of the Infinite and the Eternal. We must not be reluctant even to have the congregation hear us praying *Lord be merciful to me, a sinner* and sense the depth of our personal need. Prayer is the time for sharing woes and bearing one another's burdens —the leader must share his burdens and woes, too.

Leadership in prayer requires example, guidance, sharing, and faith; it is not for the faithless and unbelieving. Andrew Murray, in his book *With Christ in the School of Prayer,* describes the attitude which we must maintain as a leader of public prayer:

> Let us take time, as often as we pray, to listen to His voice: Everyone that asketh, receiveth. Let us not make the feeble experience of our unbelief the measure of what our faith may expect. Let us seek, not

> only just in our seasons of prayer, but at all times, to hold fast the joyful assurance: man's prayer on earth and God's answer in heaven are meant for each other.[4]

In addition to having faith in the efficacy of prayer we must also have faith in the infinite compass of God's concern. In short, we ought to lead others in prayer as a venture in faith—faith that God Almighty is willing, able, and desirous of hearing and answering our prayers.

Even if the worship leader meets the requirements of example, guidance, sharing, and faith, there will still be one thing lacking—expectation! Too often we who lead public worship have only minor expectations. Our leadership has no urgency or excitement about it because it does not spring from great expectations. We do not expect that the Holy Spirit will be at work, as we pray, acting on the pastoral yearnings we have for our people and visiting them with salvation.

Indeed, we ought to pray, as we prepare and as we present the prayer, that God will reach out through each of the prayers in the service and visit certain members of the congregation with His saving and healing power. The particularization of our expectation will quicken our sense of urgency as we lead in prayer.

Professor Hallesby describes the expectation which the Christian may have for his personal prayer life.

> The longer you live a life of this kind, the more answers to prayer you will experience. As white snow flakes fall quietly and thickly on a winter day, answers to prayer will settle down on you at every step you take, even to your dying day. The story of your life will be the story of prayer and answers to prayer.[5]

In a like manner the story of your leadership in public prayer can be the story of answers to prayer. As you have such experiences you will develop a genuine mood of expectation for your public prayers.

This theme of expectation is especially evident in the prayers of Walter Rauschenbusch. As you read his prayers you can fairly feel the expectation which motivated their composition. Notice this mood in Rauschenbusch's prayer "For Grace to Make Amends."

---

[4] Andrew Murray, *With Christ in the School of Prayer* (Westwood, N. J.: Fleming H. Revell Co., 1886), p. 37.

[5] O. Hallesby, *Prayer,* trans. Clarence J. Carlesen (Minneapolis: Augsberg Publishing House, 1944), p. 173.

> Grant us this boon, that for every harm we have done, we may do some brave act of salvation, and that for every soul that has stumbled or fallen through us, we may bring to thee some other weak or despairing one, whose strength has been renewed by our love, so that the face of Christ may smile upon us and the light within us may shine undimmed.[6]

Another way of heightening our own sense of expectation would be to use prayers (such as Rauschenbusch's) which contain this theme of expectation, both in our personal devotions and in the public services which we conduct.

PRAYER WITH THE PEOPLE

Now we turn to a consideration of the third question posed at the beginning of the chapter, "How can I pray with and for people rather than at or against them?" Assuming that every leader desires to pray with his congregation, and that his failure to do so is not a lack of intent but an inability to execute his intent, let us consider four suggestions for improving our ability to pray in this manner.

1. Increase the flexibility and responsiveness of the voice you use in leading public prayer. As indicated earlier in this chapter, a stronger voice is required for public prayer. If the leader fails to develop vocal variety and responsiveness at the level of projection required for public prayer, the strain and stiffness associated with this projection of voice may give his listeners the impression that they are being prayed *at*. Actually the leader's projection of "againstness" is a response to the demand for this additional vocal effort and not a reaction to the members of the congregation.

2. The leader must make the participation of the congregation a primary concern. Frequently leaders fall into the fallacy of thinking that their performance counts more than the congregation's participation. The leader will find it helpful to plan in terms of individual worshipers rather than in terms of the congregation as a whole.

3. The leader must have faith in the inner desire of the members of the congregation to participate in prayer. We need to have faith that God is at work in the hearts of those present, moving them to turn to Him in prayer. When we call our people to participate in the prayer of

[6] Thomas S. Kepler, *The Fellowship of the Saints* (New York: Abingdon Press, 1948), p. 585.

confession with the words, "I pray and beseech you, as many as are here present, to accompany me . . . unto the throne of Heavenly Grace,"[7] let us be especially aware of those in the congregation who are yearning to do exactly this, and who will join us in all faithfulness in the prayer of confession.

4. The leader himself must be thoroughly familiar with the prayers. It is quite unlikely that he will be able to do much to lead other people through prayers if he can hardly find his own way. Lack of familiarity may prompt the leaders to exclude any thought of other people and their needs in order to concentrate totally on the oral reading of the prayer. Familiarity with the prayers may be achieved by praying them aloud several times before praying them in the worship service. Such practice should aim at improving one's understanding and appreciation of the prayers as well as improving his oral offering of them.

Finally, the worship leader must take particular pains with such oral reading tools as grouping, pausing, and rhythm to help his hearers understand and feel the meaning of prayers. It makes a difference if, when reading the Prayer of Consecration from the communion ritual, the leader groups "Drink ye all—of this" or if he groups "Drink ye—all of this." The first grouping suggests that all are to partake; the second grouping suggests that all of the element is to be consumed by the communicant.

In connection with grouping, the duration and quality of the pauses are important. The leader should cultivate the "little pauses." Most worship leaders, for example, never bother to pause between *Almighty God* and *Our Heavenly Father,* but run both phrases together as though they were dealing with one matter which ought to be gotten out of the way as soon as possible.

The rhythm of the prayer is also important. For one thing, rhythm helps those praying to sense such varied moods as adoration, thanksgiving, and confession. Sclater declares:

> By means of rhythm, we can suggest to the mind something of the greatness which lies beyond our thought. To say "God is great" is to say something true: but the expression lies on the surface of the mind. It touches no deep spring of feeling. But if a man speaks of God as "Thou who coverest Thyself with light as with a garment," or as One "whose dwelling is the light of setting suns"; or who "inhabiteth eternity, whose Name is holy," the beat of such phrases as well as

---

[7] *The Methodist Hymnal* (New York: The Methodist Publishing House, 1939), p. 506.

their imagery, helps to express something of the sense of Divine Majesty.[8]

PRACTICE PRAYERS

In order that you might have an opportunity to apply these suggestions concerning grouping, pausing, and rhythm, the following prayers are provided for your practice reading. They pertain to four different acts of worship and provide a variety of situations for grouping, pausing, and rhythmical expression. Read them aloud, and after your first reading, make adjustments in your grouping, pausing, and rhythm. Then read them aloud again and listen for improvement. Make one more set of adjustments in grouping, pausing, and rhythm. Then read aloud a third time. In this third reading, work for abandon in the expression of the appropriate mood as well. If you have a tape recorder, tape each practice reading and then during the playback listen critically to your reading and improve your efforts.

An Invocation for the Spirit of Worship

O God our Father, open our minds that we may inquire into the beauty of Thy House of praise, open our eyes to see how lovely are Thy dwellings, open our ears to hear the present good news of Thy everlasting gospel, and open our hearts to know Thee as present Help, abiding Friend, whom we worship in spirit and in truth, through Jesus Christ our Lord.

A Prayer for Pardon

O Lord, whose mercy is from everlasting to everlasting, Thou art full of compassion and gracious, hear us in Thy mercy when we come to Thee as wayward children; renew a right spirit in us, O Lord, and restore unto us the joy we feel when we walk with Thee as children of light, strengthened for the living of these days through Christ our Lord, who has reconciled us unto Thee as Father, and in whose name we pray.

A Prayer for the Dedication of the Offering

O Christ, as wise men of old offered Thee gifts of gold and frankincense and myrrh, we too enter Thy house of prayer and present our

---

[8] J. R. P. Sclater, *The Public Worship of God* (Garden City, N. Y.: Doubleday & Company, Inc., 1927), p. 68.

gifts, the adoration of our hearts, the earnings of our hands, and the stewardship of our lives, to be consecrated by Thee, O Lord, who with the Father and the Spirit art ever worthy to be praised.

A Prayer for Hearing and Receiving the Word
(A Presermon Prayer)

Make us open, O Lord, to the word of Thy truth: may it console us in our sorrow, empower our weakness, give assurance in anxiety, judge our complacency, and confront our little lives with the power and the glory of the living Word made flesh in Jesus Christ, in whose Name we listen and preach.[9]

Now follow the same plan in your practice reading of these pastoral prayers, paying particular attention to their pattern and progression.

A Pastoral Prayer

Our gracious Heavenly Father, we do adore Thee for the beauty of the earth, for the majesty of the heavens, for the warmth of human companionship, and for the incomparable gift of Jesus Christ.

We thank Thee for this sabbath day and for the opportunity to worship Thee in this sanctuary.

Forgive us, we pray Thee, for our careless words, cruel deeds, and evil thoughts. Pardon the promotion of ourselves and the hoarding of our possessions.

Teach us to love our neighbor as ourself. Save us, we beseech Thee, from the horror of nuclear war. Have mercy upon us and lead us in the paths of peace. Help us to become peacemakers.

Heal the sick, comfort the bereaved, and visit the lonely, that our efforts to serve them may be blessed by Thy presence and Thy saving power.

Now, O Lord, we offer and present unto Thee ourselves, our souls and bodies, to be a reasonable, lively, and acceptable sacrifice unto Thee.

Hear our prayer, for we pray in the name of Jesus Christ, our Savior and Lord.

Amen.[10]

A Pastoral Prayer

O God, whose fatherliness we know through Thy being afflicted in all our afflictions and through the presence of Thine angels to com-

[9] These prayers were prepared by Alfred B. Haas, Associate Professor of Practical Theology, Drew University, Madison, N. J.

[10] This prayer was composed by the author.

fort us; whose Son we know through His suffering on the cross for our sins and through His rising again to intercede for us; whose Holy Spirit we know by the cry of *Abba, Father* in our hearts as He leads us into all truth, we praise Thee for Thy greatness, Thy goodness, and Thy grace.

Surely we should be ever mindful of Thee, our Creator, Sustainer, and Redeemer. Our motives should be purified by the thought of Thy holiness; our hearts made clean by the remembrance of Christ and His sufferings; our ambitions sanctified by a desire to do Thy will; our imaginations exalted by dwelling on the things that are above, where Christ is at Thy right hand. Thou seest how prone we are to do evil, how tardy in turning to Thee, how unfeeling in the presence of human misery, how ready to pass on the other side when our neighbor needs us. Forgive us our sins, cleanse us within by the blood of Christ, renew within us a right spirit, and enable us to discover and do Thy will.

Deepen our awareness of our dependence upon Thee, our gratefulness to Thee, our readiness to be used of Thee.

Thou hast gathered us into a great nation and extended our responsibilities to the very ends of the earth. Make us faithful to such high trust; help us to use our freedom reverently, our power justly, our resources generously, our leadership unselfishly in favor of the weak, the exploited, the oppressed, the benighted, and the despairing.

Guide our President, our legislators, counsellors, and judges with that wisdom from above which is first pure and then peaceable. Give us all a desire to please Thee and to trust Thee for the outworking of Thy wisdom and Thy will.

Enable Thy Church to be the Body of Christ, expressing His mind, serving Thy children, championing those who have no defender, bringing the glorious Good News to those who have never heard it, living as a colony of heaven, joyful in its hope and deeply rooted in love.

We pray Thy especial blessing upon us and all men in this day of divisiveness and strife. Turn us back from folly, from pride, from hastiness of judgment, and from prejudice and bitterness. Help us to understand and love those that differ from us by race or color and to realize that we are all members of Thy one family. Help us to understand how differences should enrich rather than divide and destroy, and that Christ who unites us is more important than anything that separates us.

Lift our eyes from transient things and help us to hear above the clamors of time the songs of Thy saints who have triumphed over sin and suffering, over tribulation and persecution, and whose praises are the richer because of the perils through which Thou hast brought them. With them we would worship, joining heaven and earth together in a song of praise to Thee our God, who giveth us the victory through our Lord Jesus Christ.

Amen.[11]

[11] This prayer was written by Dr. Henry L. Lambdin, Professor Emeritus of Homiletics, Drew University, Madison, N. J.

A final comment should be made about the saying of the word *Amen* to conclude the prayer. Frequently it is spoken in a voice that is barely audible or with a rising pitch—A ↗ men. The decline in force communicates uncertainty and the rise in pitch implies a question. If the decline in force and the ascent in pitch are combined, the prayer seems to conclude in the mood of an uncertain question. The speaking of the word *Amen* ought to be influenced by an interpretation of the meaning of the word itself and by the mood and meaning of the particular prayer which it concludes. It is most important that the leader's force of voice and mood of prayer be sustained through the *Amen.*

> Amen . . . is a transcription of a Hebrew word with the root idea of confirming or supporting and signifies "So be it," or "So it is." Originally it was in the nature of an affirmation of a preceding statement. By saying *Amen* the speaker made the statement his own, and said in effect "I concur." . . . In the course of time it became customary to use *Amen* at the close of public psalms, prayers or benedictions. In the New Testament epistles *Amen* occurs as the response to public or private prayers.[12]

Emphasis can be the key to a better oral interpretation of this word. Avoid emphasizing the first syllable only (*A′* men). Rather, emphasize the second syllable (A *mén*) or both syllables (*A′ mén*). As a matter of fact, the mood should not end with the second syllable of the *Amen,* but should be sustained through a brief silence following the prayer to allow and encourage the members of the congregation to complete their own personal *Amen.*

If you are familiar with the refrain to the Negro spiritual "Amen" frequently sung at summer youth camps, which is composed of a series of *Amens,* you have in the refrain a good example of putting emphasis on both syllables of the word as well as an emphatic use of the word. Just sing it and listen to the emphasis. Note also the firm, distinct enunciation of the *m* and the *n.* Say *Amen* as you have just sung it and your people will hear in it the strong affirmation that it is supposed to suggest.

---

[12] George Stimpson, *A Book About the Bible* (New York: Harper & Row, Publishers, 1945), pp. 441-42.

Chapter 13

Oral Interpretation of the Scriptures

The public reading of the Bible should not be undertaken without a previous rehearsal of the selected lesson. One of the purposes of this reading is that it shall make divine worship far more effective and reverent than it is.

S. PARKES CADMAN*

How we read the Scripture aloud depends to a considerable degree on what we believe the Scripture to be. Therefore it seems wise to begin with a review of our beliefs concerning Scripture. We believe the Bible to be the written Word of God, and as such "the sole and sufficient rule of Christian faith and practice." [1] In *Church Dogmatic I,* Barth emphasizes that although the Bible attests or points to past revelation, it only becomes the Word of God when God acts and through his action makes the Bible revelation for us here and now.

Ernest Fremont Tittle put the matter in these words,

> The Bible may be regarded as the Word of God for the reason that God makes continual use of it to bring home to men the demands of

* "The Use of the Bible in Preaching," *The Abingdon Bible Commentary* (New York: Abingdon Press, 1929), p. 43.

[1] Edwin Lewis, *Great Christian Teachings* (New York: The Methodist Book Concern, 1933), p. 14.

> His righteousness and the availability of His mercy. Reading the Bible, you may not only find yourself thinking about God, as, indeed, you can hardly avoid doing, but also you may at any moment find yourself confronted with God. Words written long ago by some prophet, psalmist, or evangelist may of a sudden become God's word to you.[2]

As a record of God's self-revelation through the history and experience of ancient Israel, the Bible both preserves and spreads a truth. It can produce in a reader the same rich experience of God that those men had who first gave us the Bible.[3]

In addition, there are certain significant analogous factors between the Bible and God's Word as it comes to us in Jesus Christ. As Jesus is God Incarnate, so in a way, the Bible, too, is God Incarnate, for God makes Himself known to us through human language and through human literary forms such as poetry, psalms, proverbs, and parables. Thus the Bible can also be regarded as both human and divine.

Such beliefs about the Bible have important implications for its oral interpretation. If we believe that the Bible is a record of the most significant series of events in all of human history, we cannot read it in a cold or detached way. Something of the value and import of what we are reading must be both audible and visible to our hearers. If we believe that as we read the Bible aloud in the worship service God himself will confront us, calling us to conform to his will and way, then it would be misleading to read the Bible in an otherworldly or "holy" tone. As we hear God's Word he invades *our* world. He confronts us where we are and in our own situation.

At this point Dietrich Bonhoeffer's comments about reading the Bible aloud seem pertinent.

> I shall be able, of course, to express the fact that it is God who is angered, who is consoling and admonishing, not by indifferent monotony, but only with inmost concern and rapport, as one who knows that it is he himself that is being addressed . . . the situation of the reader of Scripture is probably closest to that in which I read to others a letter from a friend. I would not read the letter as though I had written it myself. The distance between us would be clearly apparent as it was read. And yet I would be unable to read the letter of my

---

[2] E. F. Tittle, "On Reading the Bible," *The First Church Pulpit,* VI, No. 12 (Evanston, Illinois: The First Methodist Church, 1943), pp. 5-6.

[3] Lewis, *Great Christian Teachings,* p. 14.

> friend as if it were of no concern to me. I would read it with personal interest and regard.[4]

If we believe that the Bible is a kind of incarnation, we do not want to avoid or depreciate the human literary form, for when we neglect the artistry of the literary form, we may fail to indicate that the Bible is a truly human document. Edward Cox graphically described the danger of attempting to read the Bible in a manner different from that one would use in reading other books.

> I believe that the foundation of the fault to be a very prevalent, but very mistaken notion that the Bible requires to be read in a different manner from other books, and this independently of and in addition to the expression proper to the subject treated of. A tone is assumed that was originally designed to be reverential, as if the reader supposed that there was something holy in the words themselves apart from the ideas they express. This tone once assumed and consciously employed, but kept somewhat under control at first, soon comes to be used unconsciously and habitually. . . . The voice will unconsciously swell and fall at regular intervals, the reader all the while supposing that he is speaking quite naturally while he is really on the verge of a chant. If immediately afterward he were asked to read a narrative in a newspaper, he would do so in his own proper voice and everyday manner. This evil habit, so powerful because so imperceptible to the victim of it, is the chief mischief mainly to be grappled with, for it is the foundation of that bad reading which prevails as much in the pulpit as out of it.[5]

With this warning in mind, let us attempt to fully appreciate and communicate the artistry of the literary form in which the message is contained.

Believing that God acts to make the Bible become His Word to us as we hear it read aloud, we ought to read the Bible aloud with full anticipation of what God will do, through our reading, to minister to our people. We should read in the conviction that the read Word, like the preached Word, is a means of grace. Indeed, the read and preached Word should be thought of as being among the most significant means of redeeming and edifying the souls of men.

---

[4] Dietrich Bonhoeffer, *Life Together,* trans. John W. Doberstein (New York: Harper & Row, Publishers, 1954), p. 56.

[5] Edward W. Cox, *The Arts of Writing, Reading, and Speaking* (London: Horace Cox, 1911), p. 155.

PREPARATION FOR READING THE BIBLE ALOUD

The reader is advised to review the seven principles of preparation as they are stated and explained in Chapter 5. A good oral reading of the Scriptures requires just as much hard exegetical study as does the preparation of a good sermon.

Leaders ought to begin their preparation by reminding themselves of their goals or aims in reading the Scripture aloud. They will want both the public reading and the hearing of the Word to be an act of worship. The leader should think of his reading of the Scripture aloud as his offering to God. He should also encourage the congregation to think of their hearing of the Scripture as such an offering, for when our reading and the congregation's listening are offered to God, a new level of communication is made possible. Another aim is to have the Scriptures instruct and guide our worship. The oral reading of the Scriptures is thus viewed as an integral part of the worship service, making an essential and vital contribution to it. Still another aim for the Scripture reading is that it reaffirms the centrality of the Word of God for the illumination of our lives and the salvation of our souls. The manner and concern with which we read can suggest the vital import of God's Word for the life of every Christian.

Finally, the leader will want to share the redemption and comfort which Christians experience as they receive God's Word.

TYPES OF BIBLICAL LITERATURE

Once you are clear about your purpose, you will then want to determine which type of Biblical literature is represented by the passage which you plan to read. This is an important matter because there are several distinct types of Biblical literature—narrative, didactic, poetic, exhortative, apocalyptic, and legalistic—to name a few. In order to group words well, ascertain points of emphasis, feel the mood, and sense the rhythm, the interpreter must properly identify and fully appreciate the literary type. Obviously, this means more than a casual reflection on the matter.

Regarding Biblical prose Dr. Hunsinger observed:

> The types of prose in the . . . Bible should be studied to understand the full implication of the literature. Wisdom literature, prophetic literature, apocalyptic literature, and other less important types of prose are unique and the oral reader should know the general characteristics of each type.[6]

Professor Cobin has emphasized the importance of determining the climax when reading a narrative. He stressed the need to think of climax both in terms of impact and structure. To illustrate how one determines climax, as well as other problems in interpreting narrative literature, he makes a detailed analysis of the Biblical story of Shadrach, Meshach, and Abednego in the third chapter of Daniel.[7] This story falls into the category of political history; there are four other kinds of Biblical narrative, namely creation narratives, parables, lives of Jesus, and the history of the early church.

On the other hand, if the reader is dealing with legal prose (as found in Deuteronomy and Exodus), he needs to be aware that a group of laws will be structured with a theological introduction and conclusion.

If the passage is a unit of Old Testament poetry, literary analysis and appreciation is equally important. The reader needs to know, for example, that such poetry is dramatic, pictorial, and purposeful, with an irregular rhythm, and is regarded as a poetry of mood rather than of form. He should also be aware of the frequent use of parallelisms which can be characterized as repetitive, antithetic, and constructive. Although these parallelisms are usually thought of in connection with the psalms and prophetic literature, they can also be found in the New Testament in the teachings of Jesus.

Old Testament scholar Lawrence Toombs recommends that a reader answer the following questions when preparing to read a selection of Hebrew poetry aloud:

1. What are the significant nouns and verbs?
2. Is there any change of speaker?
3. Is there any transition from explanation to dialogue?

---

[6] Paul Hunsinger, "A Study of the Oral Interpretation of the King James Version of the Bible as the Scripture Lesson in the Sunday Morning Worship Services of the Protestant Churches," *Summary of Doctoral Dissertations, Northwestern University,* XIX (1951), p. 143.

[7] Martin Cobin, *Theory and Technique of Interpretation* (Englewood Cliffs, N. J.: Prentice-Hall, Inc., 1959), pp. 179-185.

4. What are the dramatic highlights?
5. What are the word pictures?
6. What is the poet's purpose?
7. What is the underlying mood?
8. What are the changes in mood?
9. Are there parallelisms? If so what kind?

As in the case of prose, there are several different kinds of poetry in the Bible. In his lecture "The Poetry of the Hebrews," Hugh Blair cites examples of the didactic, elegiac, pastoral, and lyric.[8]

The importance of reacquainting ourselves with such information about Biblical poetry before we attempt to read it publicly is underscored by Professor Longacre's advice concerning the reading of Biblical poetry:

> Where poems occur in the Bible . . . they should be read, not as theology, but as the free outpouring of an inspired soul who, under God, thus voices the joys and sorrows, the triumphs and defeats, of those who would otherwise remain inarticulate. More than in any other type of Biblical literature, the poems not only speak *to* man but *for* man.[9]

PLAN OF PREPARATION

The following plan, which suggests a preparation activity for each day of the week, is an attempt to apply the principles of preparation discussed in Chapter 5 to the public reading of the Scriptures. The plan begins with the Monday prior to the Sunday on which the Scripture will be read. It can, of course, be adjusted to the particularities of your assignment. You might start the plan on a different day or you might do more than one assignment a day if you have less than a week to prepare.

MONDAY — Read the passage through slowly and thoughtfully. Reread a few hours later, trying to achieve additional acquaintance with the passage.

TUESDAY — Gather pertinent literary, biographical, historical, and geographical data concerning the passage.

[8] Hugh Blair, *Lectures on Rhetoric and Belles Lettres* (London: Charles Daly, 1838), p. 568.

[9] Lindsay B. Longacre, "The Bible as Literature," *The Abingdon Bible Commentary* (New York: Abingdon Press, 1929), p. 24.

WEDNESDAY Exegete the selection using lexicon, commentaries, other translations, and similar scholarly aids.

THURSDAY Continue or review results of your exegetical study and ponder its relevance for the members of your congregation.

FRIDAY Continue to consider the passage's relevance for members of your congregation and practice reading the passage aloud.

SATURDAY Again read the passage aloud, striving for an interpretation which is adequate for the selection and for your congregation.

SUNDAY Read the selection through once and pray that your oral interpretation of it will be a fitting offering to God and that he will use it for the salvation and comfort of your parishioners.

Even though you may not be able to schedule a half hour a day for six days a week to prepare the scripture reading, this does not mean that you cannot utilize this preparation plan. Any fifteen- or twenty-minute gap during the day can be utilized for completing a phase of the plan. While waiting for a meeting to start or for a parishioner to return from surgery, you can take out a pocket Bible and get to work. Daily saturation of your mind with the Biblical selection, and reflection on it, will result in a familiarity and an understanding that will greatly improve your oral interpretation of the passage. Artistic spontaneity is the product which we desire from such daily preparation and practice of the selections which we are to read aloud.

> True spontaneity . . . does not mean an absence of deliberation, but the simultaneous action of the deliberative, the conscious and the spontaneous elements in their own proper sphere, and a co-ordinate union of them in any great impulse. It is a co-ordination of the deliberative with the unconscious that is the glory of human expression. It is the foundation of all eloquence and all poetry. In all the provinces of art it is this which is the poetic and real artistic element. Every artist must have a long, deliberative, conscious struggle to secure truthful execution, but if this struggle does not rise above technique and secure and develop the unconscious impulses of the soul, the man can never become an artist. The mechanical work is absolutely necessary, but the mechanical work alone is not sufficient, nor on the other hand, will the impulses and instincts, however strong and powerful, of themselves accomplish the result. There must be a union and co-ordination of the two, just as in nature in the lifting of the arm, there is a co-ordination of the conscious and the unconscious elements.[10]

[10] S. S. Curry, *The Province of Expression* (Boston: School of Expression, 1891), pp. 200-201.

ENRICHMENT OF YOUR APPRECIATION

In Chapter 5 the extensive opportunities in literature, music, and art for increasing one's appreciation of the Bible were mentioned. Every person who reads the Scripture publicly ought to increase his awareness and use of such resources. Moreover, if the reader has an opportunity to study Biblical Greek and Hebrew, he will discover that knowledge of Biblical languages gives him an understanding and feel for Biblical literature which is of inestimable value for oral interpretation.

Visits to museums where one may view the artifacts of Biblical times along with relief maps, partial reconstructions of buildings, drawings of cities, clothing, and events will help the reader increase the vividness of his scripture reading, because he will have visual and tactile impressions of some of the content of the selection.

Another way to enrich your appreciation for a selection is to participate in a group dramatic reading of scripture passages. Four persons might read the story of the prodigal son, with one taking the part of the prodigal, one the part of the father, one the part of the elder brother, and the fourth person reading the words of the narrator. In such reading the leader can develop a greater appreciation of how one character might have reacted to the words of another. He can also sense how the narrator participates in the story and helps move it along. In addition, the reader may find himself entering into the story more because of the stimulation of the group.

You should also regard your own oral reading and practice of the scripture lesson as a means of increasing your appreciation of its rhythm, style, and mood. This is true, in part, because of the very nature of the Scriptures, much of which were composed to be heard rather than to be read silently.

Moreover, the leader should become an avid and appreciative listener of good oral reading. Through listening to able interpreters reading aloud we can be both encouraged and inspired to improve our own efforts.

The importance of utilizing these methods for personally appreciating the scripture selection which you plan to read is forcefully stated by Dr. Curry:

> All natural expression is from within outward. It grows from cause to effect. To be natural, the reader . . . must live his message. . . . How can a reader repeat the last words of Stephen (Acts 7:37-60), recount the Jews gnashing their teeth in rage, see in imagination the hurling stones, and hear his last prayer, "lay not up this sin to their charge, "behold him gazing up into the face of his Lord and repeat this simple, sublime description, "he fell asleep"—how can any reader rehearse such events with cold neutrality and indifference! [11]

SPECIAL PROBLEMS

There are some problems in oral interpretation which are particularly prominent when reading the Scriptures. One of these pertains to the beginning and the concluding of the reading. Frequently the passage selected will be part of a longer selection, such as a part of a chapter of an epistle. The opening and closing of your selection cannot be read in the same manner as you would read these verses if you were reading the entire epistle. The first verse will have to be read with heightened intensity of meaning and mood. Likewise the last verse will have to be read in a deliberate rate and with strong projection of meaning and mood. With the opening words you need to capture attention and orient your hearers to the selection. With the concluding words you need to indicate that the reading is being completed and that the words which have been read are worth meditating.

Another problem centers around the versification and punctuation of the Bible.

> A special difficulty in the reading of the Bible arises from its division into verses and its very incorrect and imperfect punctuation. Indeed, you will find it necessary to overlook the printed signs and introduce your own pauses according to the requirements of the composition. But they very much trouble the eye, however resolved you may be not to heed them, and they certainly offer a serious impediment to good Bible reading. A still more difficult task is to pay no heed to the verses. You should so read that the listener may be unable to discover from your voice where a verse begins or ends. Often the verse is the correct measure of a sentence or a paragraph and then voice and the verse should run together, but marking it only as if it were a sentence occurring in an undivided page and with no indication of any arti-

[11] S. S. Curry, *Vocal and Literary Interpretation of the Bible* (New York: The Macmillan Company, 1903), pp. 234-35.

> ficial arrangement. The sense rarely requires this breaking up of the Bible into verses. It is a purely arbitrary arrangement. It does not exist in the original. It was adopted in translation for the convenience of reference and for chanting, and therefore there is no more call for heed to be given it in reading than if it were the history of England. Strive not to notice it. You will find the task extremely difficult, but until you have learned it, you cannot properly read the Bible aloud.[12]

In essence Cox is reminding us that we cannot be content with simply using the punctuation and grouping found in a particular edition of the Bible. Rather we must engage in our own study and interpretation, and the punctuation and grouping we use must be consonant with our findings and our interpretation.

Norma Evans Koenig underscores the importance of such an approach to the literary analysis and the oral interpretation of the scripture passage. "Unfortunately . . . we cannot always depend upon the rules of punctuation and sentence structure as rules of interpretation. Punctuation marks are like words: they are indications of meaning, but they themselves must be analyzed and interpreted." [13]

The reader will also do well to remember that the results of his work to determine the relevance of the scripture passage for his immediate congregation may also have a bearing on the punctuation of his selected passage. As Chamberlain and Clark put it,

> The ear, under guidance of the logical and rhetorical insight, gives a much more sensitive and accurate punctuation than can be indicated by printer's marks or grammarian's rules. Not the words, nor the grammatical elements, nor the customary and traditional rendering, determine grouping or inflection, but rather the speaker's purpose at the moment of utterance.[14]

A third problem arises from the content of the worship service. The reading of the Scriptures differs from the acts of preaching, praying, confession, or affirmation of faith. If the leader fails to pause, remind himself of the nature and purpose of the scripture reading, and create the mood and manner appropriate for communicating the nature and purpose of this act of worship, he will probably find himself utilizing a manner or mood more appropriate for the leadership of some other part

[12] Cox, *The Arts of Writing, Reading, and Speaking*, p. 155.

[13] Norma Evans Koenig, "The Relation of Interpretative Reading to Preaching" (Master of Arts Dissertation, University of Chicago, 1947), p. 29.

[14] W. B. Chamberlain and S. H. Clark, *Principles of Vocal Expression* (Chicago: Scott, Foresman & Company, 1897), p. 53.

of the service. Because the minister reads the worship service so frequently it becomes very familiar, and he may tend to read it mechanically without first thinking about the meaning of the words he is reading. So we need to be very wary of rushing into the reading of the scripture lesson while we still have our mind on another part of the service.

If we take Dr. Curry's advice and enjoin the truth of Scriptures upon ourselves as we read them, we may find it easier to suggest the appropriate mood for worshiping God while hearing his word:

> When a clergyman reads the Scriptures objectively, every thing appears dictatorial, or at least dogmatic or didactic; it seems as if he said to men "This truth is for you, not necessarily for me." One of the greatest teachers I ever knew once said in regard to reading the Scriptures, "You must enjoin the truth upon yourself and upon other men." Whenever the Scriptures are read without first being enjoined upon the speaker himself, whenever they are read as an intellectual lesson, merely as something for men to know, or as so many words, the performance becomes tame and flat. It inspires no realization of worship. No conception is awakened that it comes from God. . . . when the Bible is read as if the reader's heart and soul were talking with God, listening to God and feeding upon his truth, how different the effect! [15]

Finally, worship leaders labor under a heavy responsibility. Not only are they to read the Word of God aright, but they are to present it in such a way that it will feed His sheep. This is a burden which the leader should not attempt to bear alone. After he has done all he can to ready himself to read well, he must then read in the faith that God will help him to rightly discern His Word and to interpret it orally with saving power.

---

[15] Curry, *The Province of Expression,* p. 140.

Chapter 14

Oral Interpretation of the Responsive Reading

In order to read responsively, the leader must lead—he must give the cue to rhythm.

S. S. CURRY*

What should the responsive reading or the reading of the Psalter be? It should be an act of worship, consisting of the shared oral reading of God's Word, which becomes an integral part of the larger worship service.

Too many worship leaders labor under the misapprehension that this worship act may have been all right for Hebrew pilgrims who sang the psalms antiphonally as they entered the temple, but it can have little meaning and even less value for modern churchgoers. Such leaders may decry the routine, disinterested reading of the congregation without realizing that, in fact, the congregation is simply mirroring their own reading; others may hold that the members of their congregation know so little about the Bible that they are simply unable to read it well aloud. Leaders need to realize that shared oral interpretation of the Scripture presents a prime opportunity for teaching the Bible to their parishioners and for stimulating further study of it. Some leaders may find leadership of the responsive reading particularly difficult because

* *Vocal and Literary Interpretation of the Bible* (New York: The Macmillan Company, 1903), p. 330.

of the close coordination required with the participating congregation and because of the frequent use of Old Testament selections with which they lack familiarity.

Most contemporary leaders would probably place the responsive reading far down the list of the various parts of the worship service if they were asked to rate the parts in the order of their significance. They would rate the responsive reading low because they have never realized its worship potential nor achieved this potential through their own leadership.

VALUES OF RESPONSIVE READING

For such leaders of worship Dr. Curry has set forth the advantages of the responsive reading in the worship service:

> It brings members of the congregation into union with each other and with the leader, and causes all to participate in worship. It gives all a feeling that they have something to do, and tends to banish altogether the idea, too prevalent, that men come to church for mere instruction or to be merely interested.
>
> Responsive reading is a great aid to the preacher also, and helps him to forget himself and to feel himself a part of the assembly. It gives him a chance to awaken the minds of his congregation. . . . [1]

The responsive reading also enables the leader to help the congregation worship. Through the responsive reading, the leader is able to offer the congregation the opportunity, the words, and the encouragement to orally express their adoration, thanksgiving, confession, petitions, and dedication to God. Some people do not have the words to use or the opportunity or encouragement for putting their religious experiences and yearnings into words. They benefit greatly from the responsive reading, through which they can give expression to vital religious experiences and desires.

The responsive reading, too, is a fruitful way to teach worshipers the Bible. In reading the Bible aloud, the reader is helped to understand and appreciate both its intellectual and emotional content. By guiding the congregation, the worship leader can suggest the mood of the selection, the rhythm of the passage, and the manner in which words should

[1] S. S. Curry, *Vocal and Literary Interpretation of the Bible* (New York: The Macmillan Company, 1903), pp. 328-29.

be grouped and emphasized. Each of these factors indicates something of the selection's meaning and mood. Moreover, if the worshiper finds the reading interesting, helpful, or provocative, he will very likely seek out the Biblical passage and study it more carefully.

Responsive reading can also stimulate our desire to enter into worship. The worshiper has the guidance of a leader, the companionship and stimulation of the congregation, and the riches of the word of God to touch his heart and stir his soul. In addition, he has the motivation of all the preceding elements of the worship service.

The worship leader needs to be aware of the significant worship and educational purposes which the responsive reading can fulfill; then he needs to fulfill one of these purposes through the shared oral reading of the Bible in each worship service which he leads. In striving for this achievement, one might become an effective worship leader. He might take up boldly the role described by David W. Thompson:

> The role is that of initiator in two senses of the word. He initiates, or begins, the empathic response to the literary work. He initiates, or inducts, the audience into the society of sharers in the total imaginative experience! He leads them in responding to the work, and he leads them to a membership in it.[2]

LEADERSHIP METHODS

The primary method is the attempt to share the meaning of the responsive reading. The congregation is moved to worship God by their shared understanding of the meaning of the selection. Like the scripture lesson, the responsive reading instructs and guides the worshiper. We are moved to praise and adore God as we are informed about His wisdom, His majesty, and His loving kindness. As a matter of fact, the responsive reading is frequently used as the Old Testament lesson or as the reading from the Epistles. Consequently, the leader must prepare to read the responsive selection with the same thoroughness that he prepares to read the scripture lesson. Let it be clearly understood that the leader cannot hope to lead the congregation into a meaningful worship experience unless he himself thoroughly comprehends and appreciates the selection. The section of the preceding chapter entitled

---

[2] David W. Thompson, "Interpretative Reading as Symbolic Action," *The Quarterly Journal of Speech*, XLII, No. 4 (1956), p. 391.

"Preparation for Reading the Bible Aloud" should be carefully reviewed and it should be used as a guide in preparing the responsive reading. The leader should have the same keen desire to share the meaning of the responsive reading as he has to share the meaning of the sermon or meditation. Far too many worship leaders make no preparation of the responsive reading. Many do not even read it through aloud before the service. In short, most worship leaders do not know or appreciate the responsive reading selection, and this is a shameful way to attempt to share the Word of God with their people.

The leader should give clear, emphatic indication of the rhythm of the reading. After a common understanding of meaning, a common appreciation of the rhythm of the selection is the second strongest factor contributing to the orderliness of a unison reading. Although some adjustments in rate may be required by the size of the congregation, degree of appreciation for the responsive reading, and like matters, the rhythm must be primarily determined by the meaning and mood of the selection which is being read.

Where meaning, mood, or both indicate a change in rhythm at some point in the selection, the leader must change the rhythm of his reading promptly at the appropriate time. When in the first Psalm we turn to a consideration of the ungodly, a new rhythm is called for because a different meaning and mood are now to be communicated. If the reading continued in the same rhythm, the contrast between the godly and the ungodly man would be diminished. Further help in the use of rhythm can be obtained by referring to the section on rhythm in Chapter 9.

Another question related to the matter of rhythm is this: "How shall I determine when to start reading my lines after the congregation has read theirs?" The meaning and mood of the selection are primary concerns, and no method should be utilized without regard for them. The leader should always take a full breath just prior to starting to read, and should avoid rushing or crowding the congregation. As Dr. Curry reminds us,

> All depends on the way responsive readings are conducted. When they are given in the right spirit, the leader can interpret the thought and feeling of his line or verse. The rush and whirl are not necessary, and people may be inspired to read with sincerity and not to repeat as a mere formality.[3]

---

[3] Curry, *Vocal and Literary Interpretation of the Bible,* p. 329.

One way of preserving spontaneity as well as achieving a certain rhythm of response is for the leader to take a full breath during the last phrase which the congregation reads, then start to read as he feels moved by the selection's meaning and mood to do so. The way the congregation handles the responses will also tend to prompt you in initiating your section. If the congregation has become involved in the reading, their involvement will stimulate your leadership. In order to be so prompted or stimulated, the leader must give some attention to how the congregation is responding and become sensitive to how they are being moved and informed by the reading. A reader who is only concerned about how he is reading will not be cued by the congregation to initiate his verses. If the leader is discriminating in listening to the congregation's participation, he may hear several levels of response. The reading may have different meaning and impact for the aged than for the teen-ager, or for those who have gone through hardships as compared to those who have experienced easy times.

Madeline L'Engle points out that a good children's book has many levels:

> Another constant in good children's books is that they are many-leveled. It doesn't matter that we understand only the surface of Alice's adventure when we are only 8; that at 18 we discover Lewis Carroll has all kinds of wise and wondrous things to say about human nature, not to mention the politics of Victorian England—and that later, when we read "Alice" with an 8-year-old son who is learning chess, we suddenly catch on to all the fun of the chess game that is played more or less, all through Alice's adventures through the Looking Glass. It is these multiple levels, as transparent and delicate as the layers of the French pastry, *mille feuilles,* that cause a child to return to a good book over and over again.
>
> Good books have infinite variety and infinite capacity for being reborn.[4]

The Bible has infinite variety and infinite capacity for being reborn. It is many-leveled and all members of the congregation can read it aloud together with profit and pleasure week after week. The leader will give better leadership to the responsive reading if he is immediately aware of the congregation's involvement in the reading and of how its members are being instructed and moved by it. Insofar as he shares the wor-

[4] Madeline L'Engle, "How's One to Tell?," *The New York Times Book Review,* May 12, 1963, p. 1.

ship experience with them he will be given invaluable clues for the initiating of his portions of the reading.

An equally important factor is the way the leader concludes his parts of the reading. The concluding words must not sound as though he is trailing off or fading away. Frequently this is just the way the leader's parts of the reading are concluded, and this habit destroys the congregation's enthusiasm for reading well. The leader may avoid this fault by replenishing his breath supply with an appropriate pause and by emphasizing one of the words in the concluding phrase. It is most important that we do not fall into habitual or mechanical ways of concluding sections of the reading. For example, some readers have developed the habit of raising the pitch of their voices for every sentence that is punctuated with a question mark.

> If there is one punctuation mark which is never taught correctly, it is the interrogation point. One feels that life is not long enough to overcome the bad habit attained in school of thinking that this mark indicates a rising inflection. As soon as students can see a question mark on a printed page, they begin to ascend the vocal scale. The question mark indicates a rising inflection only about once in one thousand times. The motive, the meaning, governs the melody or the pitch.
>
> If there is one punctuation mark we feel sure of interpreting, it is the question mark. But are we interpreting it? Does the question mark always mean that the speaker asks for information? No! Grammatically, the question mark indicates an interrogative sentence. It is not the grammar but the purpose which determines the vocal expression.[5]

We have only to recall the psalmist's words—"What is man that Thou art mindful of him"—to feel the force of these observations.

In addition to reading the interrogatives well, the leader must avoid concluding thoughts which are continued in the following congregational response. In some instances the leader's part will end with a colon and he will have fair warning. At other times he will have to be guided by the meaning and purpose of the author. Realizing that the concluding words of each unit will cue the congregation as to how they should read their unit, the leader must read these words particularly well with the aim of evoking good oral reading from the congregation.

---

[5] S. H. Clark and Maud May Babcock, *Interpretation of the Printed Page* (Englewood Cliffs, N. J.: Prentice-Hall, Inc., 1940), pp. 160-61.

Another important requirement of leadership for the responsive reading is the growth in intensity of leadership as the reading progresses. If the leadership wanes or levels off, the congregational response will do likewise. Through his own involvement in the reading, the leader must overcome any feelings of fatigue or boredom. If the leader will concentrate on communicating with a particular person by reaching out to this person through his reading and encouraging him to enter into the reading, he himself may find it easier to become more involved in the reading as it progresses. Especially will this be true if he notices some signs of response and participation from the person for whom he is particularly concerned.

However, this suggestion is not meant to serve as a substitute for careful analysis of the verses being read and the way they are ordered—with an aim to determining the climax of the selection as well as the steps leading up to it. If such an analysis has been made, an awareness of the pastoral possibilities of this act of worship may help the leader maintain his interest and strengthen his leadership effort.

Then, too, the leader might quicken his appreciation and eagerness to participate in the responsive reading if he would reflect on its position as a part of the ancient tradition of the church through which we are privileged to worship even as did the prophets, Our Lord Himself, and the early Christian martyrs.

Finally, he might reflect anew on the way in which this worship act contributes to a strong congregational consciousness in our worship. Elmer Leslie emphasizes the importance of this aspect in his discussion of the psalms:

> The religion of the psalms is a communion, a sharing between the human and the divine. And the thing that lifts this communion, great as it is in itself, to something yet nobler and more potent is that it is communion with God in fellowship with other men. For always behind the experience of the psalmist, undergirding it and buoying it up, is the social fellowship of the congregation.[6]

A good selection to read for practice is Psalm 24, one of the liturgies of entrance to the holy place. In this psalm the question-answer sequence dramatizes leadership and response, so that the leader involuntarily enters more and more fully into the antiphonal nature of the psalm. This

---

[6] Elmer A. Leslie, *The Psalms* (New York: Abingdon Press, 1949), p. 18.

is particularly true of verses seven through ten. By practicing with a selection where you sense more readily the appropriateness of alternation in reading, you may later read with more skill those passages where the appropriateness of the divisions is not so immediately apparent.

Chapter 15

Oral Interpretation of Hymns and Religious Poetry

Poetry may be said to be the particular province of the oral interpreter because it reaches its ultimate objective only when it is read aloud.

CHARLOTTE I. LEE*

The leader may enrich the worship service in several different ways by reading hymns aloud. He may read part of a hymn aloud to the congregation prior to their singing it, in order to encourage them to think about the meaning of the words as they sing. He may read a portion of a hymn as a call to worship. Occasionally a leader will read the words of a hymn as a prayer. (A large number of hymns are prayers.) Then, too, parts of hymns are quoted in meditations and sermons. Many pastors read hymns at funeral services. In these and other ways the leader will find that by improving his ability to read hymns aloud he has opened opportunities for enriching the leadership of worship services.

An important consideration in the oral reading of hymns is the reading of meaning rather than melody or meter. When these last two factors appropriately coincide with the meaning they can be utilized to reinforce it. However, the melody or meter must never be allowed to substitute for the meaning or overshadow it.

In order to avoid any such error, some leaders make it a practice to

---

* *Oral Interpretation* (Boston: Houghton Mifflin Company, 1952), p. 427.

copy the words of the hymns on a separate sheet of paper so that their reading will not be unduly influenced by the musical score. In making a copy they are also able to group the words according to meaning rather than according to the distribution of notes on the hymnal page.

Another inclination to be overcome is the tendency to emphasize all the rhyming words. If, according to the intellectual and emotional content of the hymn, the emphasis falls appropriately on a rhymed word, the reader should so emphasize it. However, the word should not be emphasized to call attention to the rhyme. The reader should certainly avoid a mechanical emphasis of all rhymed words, for this will probably result in calling attention to rhyme at the expense of meaning.

The hymn must be read as a complete work. It may be that a thought continues directly from the end of one stanza into the beginning of the next. A marked break or pause, as we might customarily observe in the singing of the hymn, would be an inappropriate interruption for an oral interpretation of the hymn. Meaning and mood may well necessitate ignoring one of these major divisions in the hymn. The metrical version of the Twenty-Third Psalm provides a good example of this problem (see hymn No. 70 in *The Methodist Hymnal*).

PRECONDITIONING THE AUDIENCE

Just as the leader may have previous associations of the words of the hymn (certain melody patterns, rhythms, rhymes, and divisions), so the audience may be accustomed to hearing the words of the hymn in a similar context. When the leader reads a hymn aloud with the intent of focusing the hearer's attention on the meaning of the words, he has to get the congregation to listen to the hymn in a new or different way.

Consequently, he himself must have a very vivid comprehension of the meaning of the hymn. If the leader goes at the matter seriously, he will frequently discover that he has been singing hymns for as long as he can remember without ever knowing or understanding their true or full meaning. In seeking to intensify the meaning of the hymn for himself, the leader should follow the study methods suggested in Chapter 2 to help him become better acquainted with the meaning of the hymn.

Some hymns, like the metrical version of the Twenty-Third Psalm and the following hymn, are a paraphrase or restatement of a Biblical passage.

O Lord our Master, all the earth
Thy majesty proclaims,
The lamps of heaven each night give worth
To what Thou hast ordained.

We can but gaze with rev'rent eyes
Upon the moon's soft rays;
The storm-clouds driven through the skies,
Are vocal with thy praise.

O Lord our Master, what is man
That Thou shouldst care for him?
This creature, measured by a span,
Dost Thou remember him?

Yea, care Thou must, for Adam's breed
In pow'r hath been enthroned;
All living things on earth that feed
Are ruled by man alone.

O Lord our Master, earth and heaven
Declare their Maker's praise.
Can man, to whom so much is given,
Neglect his voice to raise?

Alfred B. Haas

This paraphrase of the Eighth Psalm may be sung to Dundee. Being a paraphrase, real comprehension and appreciation of its meaning would require the same sort of investigation and reflection recommended in Chapter 13, *Oral Interpretation of the Scriptures.* Particular attention should be given to the questions suggested by Dr. Toombs.

Not only must the reader have a particularly vivid impression of the hymn's meaning, but he must also be especially effective in his oral interpretation of it if he wishes to overcome the congregation's preconditioned response to these words. The new grouping, emphasis, and melody pattern must be deliberate, vigorous, and firm. The voice ought to be clear and well projected, the articulation distinct, and the reading done without any indecision or hesitation. Abandon and freedom in oral expression will be a genuine aid to the congregation in listening to the hymn in a new manner. Effective oral reading of hymns requires special care both in preparation and presentation.

In addition, the reader will be aided by an ability to distinguish between German chorales, English hymns, and American church songs, and also by an appreciation of their particular merits and significant characteristics. For quickening his appreciation of and gaining more knowledge about hymns, the leader should consult such sources of information as:

Our Hymnody by R. G. McCutchen (1937). Methodist Publishing House, Nashville, Tennessee.

The Hymn, a quarterly publication by the Hymn Society of America, 475 Riverside Drive, New York 27, New York.

A Survey of Christian Hymnody by William Reynolds (1963). Holt, Rinehart and Winston, Inc., 383 Madison Ave., New York 17, N. Y.

The Gospel in Hymns by A. E. Bailey (1950). Charles Scribner's Sons, 597 Fifth Ave., New York 17, N. Y.

READING RELIGIOUS POETRY

Let us recognize at the outset that the texts of hymns are indeed religious verse. The hymns have been treated separately in order that particular observations could be made about them as a group. Because hymns are religious poetry, much of the advice given about the oral reading of hymns applies to the oral interpretation of religious poetry as well. Moreover, some of the advice given on the reading of Biblical poetry in Chapter 13 also pertains to a general discussion of the oral reading of religious poetry. The following remarks pertain more to the oral reading of religious poetry which is found neither in the Bible nor the Hymnal. On the other hand, these remarks may have important implications for the reading of Biblical poetry and hymns.

ORIENTATING ONESELF TO POETRY

It is most important that the reader have a keen awareness of how the poet seeks to stir our imagination, arouse our emotions, and move us along with the rhythm of the poem. Poetry is suggestive. It seeks to set our minds wondering and wandering. Notice how Stoneburner's poem sweeps you along with its rapid movement, triggers your imagination, and touches your feelings, and sets your mind wondering.

Hosea VICTOR Waiting for David VICTOR.

This year the old man, dwindled in the flesh
Upon his skeleton, could not contain
Himself. He waited for the child who dwelt
Elsewhere. And when the child—flesh of his flesh,
Bone of his bone—appeared, and only then,
The great grandfather was at home, the child
Sat in the ancient lap at ease to force
Sweets in the ruined mouth. The old man smiled
As dryness watered and hard candy melted.
I thought of Simeon whose decrepitude
Was sacred, good for nothing but to yearn
For God, and yield to Him. Once his frail hands
Had held the small one to his breast, he was
Content to die.

Tony Stoneburner

Because poetry deals in such things as imagination, emotion, suggestion, and rhythm, it usually has fuller communicative potential than other types of literature. Most of us have difficulty in reading poetry aloud because we do not give ourselves to the communicating of the wholeness of the poem—its total meaning and wider implications. We read poetry with the same rate and limited range of expression which we use in reading other types of literature.

When attempting to read poetry aloud, we would do well to keep before us Ben Henneke's advice to radio announcers concerning the communication of emotion:

> Every word has resulted from the need to express a sensation or concept, and many are pregnant with emotion and associative implications as well as meaning.
>
> The announcer should re-create in his imagination the emotional sensations suggested by the word he reads. He should see in his mind's eye the picture the copy visions. He should hear the sounds, and smell the odors, and feel the tactile sensations embodied in his announcements. Just as the announcer must understand an idea before his listener can, so the announcer must sense before the listener can.
>
> . . . One of the duties of an announcer is to revive for the listener the emotional value of words.[1]

[1] Ben G. Henneke, *The Radio Announcer's Handbook* (New York: Holt, Rinehart & Winston, Inc., 1948), p. 15.

One way to achieve fuller expression of the meaning of poetry is to make use of our full pitch range and to strive for more abandon in responding to variations in meaning with variations in pitch. This should not be achieved in a mechanical manner but in terms of fuller vocal responsiveness to what we understand and feel about the poem. If we are fully alert to the occasion, physically rested, and concentrating intently on the selection, we should experience a certain natural improvement in terms of the pitch variations or vocal melody.

Few readers are sufficiently aware of the vital role which pitch plays in the oral interpretation of poetry. Invariably the communication of the finer shades of mood and meaning require subtle variations in pitch. Moreover, changes in pitch complement poetic rhythm and contribute to the effects produced by poetic rhythm.

One way of achieving greater vocal expression in terms of pitch or melody pattern would be to read the poem aloud and emphasize the rise and fall of pitch. The reader might deliberately exaggerate changes in pitch as a way of becoming aware of the need for use of pitch variations; it is also a way of limbering up the vocal mechanism for fuller expression through variation in pitch.

The need to avoid habitual or mechanical pauses, such as a pause at the end of each line, was discussed earlier in this chapter in connection with the oral reading of hymns. As such faulty use of pauses would be equally detrimental to other types of religious verse, we would do well to consider the remarks of Edward Cox on the misuse of the pause:

> Avoid set pauses. Some readers, otherwise skilful, will make a pause at precisely the same point in the meter of each line, whether the sense does or does not require it. This is not merely monotonous—it is wrong. In the reading of poetry, as of prose, the sound must be subordinate to the sense. Although there is a measuring of the words in poetry, there is no measure for the pauses. You must pause wheresoever the sense demands a pause, without regard to the apparent exigencies of meter or rhyme. If that pause so falls that it disturbs the melody of the verse or the harmony of the rhyme, you should preserve them by so managing your voice that, after the pause, it shall resume with the selfsame tone with which it rested, just reminding the hearer of the music of the verse as an added charm to the beauty of the thought. Then, again, shun carefully the still more frequent practice of pausing at the end of each line, regardless of the requirement of the thought.[2]

[2] Edward Cox, *The Arts of Writing, Reading, and Speaking* (London: Horace Cox, 1911), p. 139.

Pauses must be prompted by our involvement and response to the poetry we are reading aloud. They cannot be habitual or programmed ahead of time and then mechanically executed at the time of public reading. Suppose that a reader who inserted a pause after the rhyme at the end of each line and at the same point in the middle were asked to read the following contemporary religious poem aloud:

TABULATOR

a great multitude which no man can number
of all nations and kindreds and people and tongues
which our exacting God can tally
by calculation and catalogues
as he is able to audit each entry
of the multiple volumes of the Book of Life
one in a thousand but by the hundreds
tears in bottles   tossings in bed
flying sparrows falling and dying
needle in haystack   hairs on head
coin in corner   lamb in hillcountry
homecoming spendthrift son
rejoicing angels dancing on pin point
how many?   how many?
ecstatic statistics   love

Tony Stoneburner

Not only would such habits of pausing stand a reader in poor stead when attempting to read a poem like "Tabulator," but they would also tend to stifle any effort to interpret poetry orally in a meaningful and moving way. Rhythm is such an important factor in the reading of poetry that it ought not to be erased by a habit of pausing at regular intervals when reading verse aloud.

In the reading of contemporary poetry a habit of pausing like the one cited above would cut across the form of free verse and mask its design. As Melville Cane observes:

> The very nature of the modern poet's enterprise seems to call for free verse and the subordination of rhyme. Paradoxically, free verse to be successfully employed must obey its own laws of form and design. Its freedom is not absolute but comparative. In the hands of its most competent users one always senses the presence of an underlying control. Pegasus is still directed in his flights but with a looser rein.[3]

[3] Melville Cane, "Are Poets Returning to Lyricism?" *The Saturday Review*, January 1954, p. 9.

SHARING THE BEAUTY OF POETIC FORM

Although the thrust of this chapter has been to urge the reader to undergird himself with a full, rich appreciation of the meaning of poetry, remember that the form, rhythm, rhyme, and melody also must be shared, for they are part of what and how the poem means and feels. The reader must communicate an appreciation for the artistic way *in which* the poem speaks as well as *for what* it speaks. In reading the following poem, take note of how the rhythm, grouping, and alliteration contribute to the poem's meaning and mood.

JESUS

Lover of the lowly,
Helper of the humble,

Saviour of the sinner,
Cleanser of the corrupt,
Redeemer of the wretched,

Forgiver of the faithless,

Succourer of the sorrowing,
Shepherd of the suffering,
Companion of the cursed,

Healer of the hurt,
Light of the lost,

Gift of God.

Harold A. Brack

SHARING THE PLEASURE OF POETRY

In the last analysis, the most helpful thing a reader can do to improve his reading of poetry is to read poetry aloud frequently to various persons and groups until he begins to experience a sharing of the pleasure which he himself finds in the poetry. When he knows that others are sharing the appreciation and delight which he is now experiencing, he will find himself interpreting with great freedom and fullness of expression. With that aim in mind, you are urged to read aloud to others the hymns and poems which appear on the previous pages of this chapter as well as those that follow, attempting to share the pleasure which you yourself find in reading them.

MEDITATION ON GRACE
Beatitudo, C.M.

Great searcher of the secret heart,
  Thou knowest what our grief,
When struggle only arms the self,
  From which we seek relief.

Lord Christ, uplifted on the cross,
  We bring our hearts to Thee,
Whose grace, abounding more than sin,
  Flows measureless and free.

Make clean the well-springs of desire,
  Our mind's aspirings claim,
Create fresh hunger for Thy word,
  New joy to hear Thy name.

We turn from self, we turn from sin,
  Our captive hearts set free;
Empow'rer of the contrite soul,
  Our strong salvation be.

Henry Lyle Lambdin

COME, LET US SEEK THE KINGDOM
Webb 7,6,7,6,D

Come, let us seek the Kingdom
  Our Master has begun,
By whom, as we beheld Him,
  The Father's will was done.
Through His sublime obedience
  Christ made the Kingdom His,
And where men have His spirit
  The Heavenly Kingdom is.

Come, let us work together,
  Neath God's eternal plan
That justice, truth and freedom
  Join man to fellow man;
Forgiving since forgiven,
  Our goal the common Good,

Our Risen Lord as Leader
His Church one Brotherhood.

Come, let us join the blessed
Who choose the better part;
The meek, the poor in spirit,
The sad, the pure in heart,
The peacemakers, the righteous,
All prophet souls who bear
A true and faithful witness,
The Heavenly Kingdom share.

Come, let us seek the Kingdom
For which we daily pray,
The realm like unto Heaven
Where God holds perfect sway;
In faith that looks not backward,
In faith that works by love,
In faith that trusts His promise,
And bids the mountains move.

Henry Lyle Lambdin[4]

THE WEAVER

*"Ach, ich soll Stroh zu Gold
spinnen und verstehe das doch gar
nicht."
"Was gibt du mir, wenn ich
dir's spinne?"* [5]

—*Gebr. Grimm:* Rumpelstilzchen

*He who dwells among the lilies
reigns above the stars.*

—Bernard of Clairvaux

Yonder above
Where the moon weaves
Wonder of stars, and of starlight!
Starlight shredded,
Shredded down—like thistle down,
Like thistle seeds

---

[4] From a collection of unpublished hymns by Dr. Henry Lyle Lambdin. Reprinted by permission. All rights reserved by Dr. Henry Lyle Lambdin.

[5] "Alas, I must spin straw into gold
and I do not understand it at all."
"What will you give me
if I spin it for you?"

That float on high in a light wind
Downward—softly and down
To the stubble:
Yonder above
Where the moon weaves
Straw into gold for the Kingdom,
There *is* the Kingdom!
Kingdom of God,
And *my* kingdom.

There too is Christ,
Our Jesus!—shining!
Glory like stars!—and weaving!
Behold how he weaves,
Him weaving,
Straw of our sorrows
To gold thread, weaving—
Fine-spun and thin-spun,
Gossamer, golden,
Now, and again,
And forever again
For the Kingdom!

For this *is* the Kingdom
Where the Light shines
And the Christ weaves
And the petulant straw
Of our kingdoms,
Dominions of sorrow,
Is woven to gold
For the Kingdom.

Yonder above
Where the white sheaves
Stand in the moonlight and glisten—
Straw white sheaves
Of our sorrow—
There Jesus weaves!
Christ weaving! [6]

Stanley Romaine Hopper

[6] From a collection of unpublished poems by Dr. Stanley Romaine Hopper. Reprinted by permission. All rights reserved by Dr. Stanley Romaine Hopper. Dr. Hopper suggests that when "The Weaver" is read aloud the reader be alert for the spinning rhythm.

SEABURY SPIRE

Graceful, slender, piercing the sky,
Swiftly, skillfully, lifting the eye,
Sending the soul, soaring free
To cross, cloud, and Thee.

Harold A. Brack

COME TO ME WAVES

Come to me, waves—
come rushing at me
with ocean-sweeping force.

I shall stand stone-still,
face full forward
until the end

when I am washed up
on the shore,
polished.

Marilyn Plowman

GOD'S CHRISTMAS GIFT

God's Christmas gift to the crying world
was thrust from the warm mother womb
and wrapped in binding white swaddling cloths—

and loosed from binding white burying cloths
was thrust from the cold stone-closed tomb,
God's Easter gift to the crying world.

Marilyn Plowman

IN SICKNESS

Through the quiet darkness of the waning night,
A lonely prayer ascends in desperate flight.
"If this body Thou will not heal,
Then into death let me quickly steal.

Wasting limbs have I hopefully born,
While flesh with torturing pain is torn,
And fever consumes like a thirsting flame.
Lord, release me, in Thy good Son's name.

But if this request, Thou will deny,
And in agony I still must lie,
Then grant me strength and loving art,
That I may boast a cheerful heart!"

Harold A. Brack

CAN YOU NOT WATCH?

"Can you not watch with me
a while?"
He cries out.

No,
they have fled;
there are none watching
the city streets are deserted,

except for one lonely policeman
who has stopped to watch
the Easter chicks
huddled together
in the petstore window.

But they need no watching
for their cage is closed up tight
and they have their light
to keep them
warm.

Marilyn Plowman

PART FOUR: ORAL INTERPRETATION OF THE RITUAL

Chapter 16

Oral Reading of the Ritual

*The visible church of Christ is a congregation of faithful men in which the pure Word of God is preached, and the sacraments duly administered according to Christ's ordinance.**

An able oral reading of the ritual makes a very considerable contribution to the due administration of the sacraments. It is equally important for reverent and meaningful funeral and wedding services. This chapter will set forth several suggestions for improving your oral interpretation of the ritual. Subsequent chapters will deal in detail with the ritual for baptism, communion, matrimony, and burial of the dead. The content of this chapter pertains to the reading of these four services as well as such events as the reception of members, the consecration of church workers and officers, the dedication of church buildings and equipment, and like events in the life of the church.

---

* *Doctrine and Discipline of the Methodist Church* (New York: The Methodist Publishing House, 1948), pp. 27-28.

AVOID MECHANICAL READING

Several factors seem to conspire to make the minister prone to a habitual and mechanical reading of the ritual.

1. In a large measure he is reading exactly the same words over and over again.

2. The minister prepares in a much more limited way for the reading of these services than he does for the Sunday worship service. In part, this is due to his viewing of these services as tasks of secondary importance. In the case of the funeral service, he only has about forty-eight hours from the time of notification to the time of the service; frequently most of his time has already been committed for other tasks. Or, in the case of the wedding rehearsal, the minister has little, if any, opportunity to practice his reading of the ritual during the rehearsal.

3. The amount of material to be read makes men fear that they will be uninteresting. Hence they read more rapidly than their natural rate to prevent the service from dragging.

4. The minister frequently focuses a good part of his attention on the acts of leadership related to the ritual and therefore does not fully attend to the words as he reads.

5. Some leaders maintain a certain detachment in order to avoid becoming distracted by the individuals to whom they are administering the sacraments. This effort to read in a detached manner often suggests to the congregation that the leader is aloof or disinterested. The following suggestions are intended to help the minister successfully combat these influences toward a mechanical reading.

Every minister needs to make a thorough, detailed, personal study of each part of the ritual. He should have a clear and complete knowledge of its Biblical and theological content. In addition, he should know its historical antecedents and how and why it has evolved to its present state. The minister should also be completely familiar with the over-all design of each order, including an awareness of the climax and the way in which the various parts contribute to the climactic progression.

Henry Ward Beecher's description of how the phrases of prayer contribute to the whole suggests how we might view a worship service:

> While prayer may consist of any or all of these elements, ordinarily they will mingle with or succeed each other, the soul ranging from

> one feeling to another. Each step prepares you for the next. The confession of sin introduces a thought of benignity. That enkindles gratitude; and often we come almost unconsciously from an acknowledgment of our unworthiness to the act of praising God. The expression of thanks calls up ideas of Divine goodness and glory, so that the soul cannot but experience admiration. When this is softened by veneration it is simple worship; when it is also enriched by love it is adoration. In any comprehensive Christian experience that utters itself in prayer, confession, supplication, communion, thanksgiving, and praise come and go and blend to form the great whole, as do the tones of different instruments in a well-chorded orchestra. In other words, prayer is the simple interchange of thought and feeling with God; rising out of conscious sensuousness into spirituality: turning one's self away from the things of time, and standing on the threshold of the eternal world.[1]

The leader should know each word of the service he is conducting. He should know the word's total meaning and not be content with a vague idea of its meaning. In order to test the adequacy of your own knowledge of the specific words in each ritual, write a brief definition for each of the following words:

Communion

charity	partake
bewail	beseech
advocate	oblation
propitiation	grievous
contrite	property (his)
bounden	presume
remission	meet (it is very meet, right . . .)

Baptism

consecrated	solemn
steadfast	admonition
precept	supplication
lo	

Reception of Members

edification	discretion
thereto	

Matrimony

estate	haven
plight	asunder
cherish	avail

[1] Henry Ward Beecher, *A Book of Public Prayer* (Westwood, N. J.: Fleming H. Revell Co., 1892), p. 10.

Burial

corruptible
consummation
cleaving
mediator
countenance (his)
henceforth

Now, with a good dictionary and a copy of the ritual, correct your definitions. It may be that as you work through the list you will notice other words in the ritual for which you could not write clear or accurate definitions. If your own understanding of a word is vague, you will not be able to interpret the word clearly to others.

In addition to knowing the meaning of words, you must also know their pronunciation. A few examples of common mistakes are cited here to warn you that you may need to examine your own pronunciation.

1. The word *saith* is mispronounced as *sāyeth* instead of *seth.*
2. The word *brethren* is mispronounced as *brothern* instead of *brethren.*
3. The *un* prefix is mispronounced so that the word *unto* sounds like *onto.*
4. The consonant *t* in the word propi*t*iation is mispronounced as *t* instead of *sh.*
5. The word *grievous* is mispronounced as *gre ve us* instead of *gre vus.*

Once the minister knows the meaning of a word and how to pronounce it, he will be in a better position to interpret it orally to others.

A keen awareness of the divisions of the ritual is vital to effective leadership. The leader must be aware of the various types of religious literature involved, such as addresses to the congregation, prayers, Scriptures, vows, and benedictions. In addition, the minister should be aware of the different persons to whom the ritual may be directed. It may be addressed to a single individual, to a small group, to the entire congregation, or to God. Awareness of these distinctions should have an effect on our oral reading of the ritual. The parts should have varied moods and move at different rates and with different degrees of force.

The minister must also understand and appreciate the potential of the ritual for converting the occasion into a sacred event in the lives of the participants. He must know how this particular order can lead people into the kind of worship experience described by Roger Hazelton:

> Worship is the supreme moment of human life. It achieves its own interest whenever it makes possible the awesome contact between God

> and man. It brings together our upward longing and striving with the descending love of the divine. In that moment a vision of splendor and delight possesses us, and "the world is charged with the grandeur of God." Yet even as we are lifted, we are cast down. When we behold what God is, we learn most clearly what we are. Thus we are taught to put our trust in Him, that He may work within us that which is well pleasing in his sight. In worship the spirit of God bears witness with our spirit, that we are children of God.[2]

It is the purpose of the ritual to lift these events—communion, baptism, marriage, and burial—to the level of the sacred. The participants need to be given a vision of what these experiences can be if they are entered into with God and if they proceed in accord with God's will. Seward Hiltner reminds us that ". . . we have in all Protestant churches particular acts which may have a meaning deeper than words —not only because of their age but also because they symbolize the relation between fundamental religious truth and the most common acts of life."[3]

Consequently the oral interpretation of the ritual must be personal rather than impersonal. It must be read for the needs of those persons who are now participating in the service. Moreover, you ought to have goals which you are praying to God you may achieve in the lives of these persons by sharing the ritual with them.

SHARE THE EXPERIENCE

The ritual must be a shared entrance into the presence of God. We take some of the congregation apart with us as we pray even as Jesus took Peter, James, and John apart with Him in the garden where He prayed. In turn, we and this smaller group share the event with the whole congregation. Indeed, the congregation is to be ministered unto as well as those persons immediately involved. This will mean abandon in vocal expression and projection. It will mean interpreting the ritual with an open heart and soul, and a vivid awareness of the individuals present—their needs, yearnings, hopes, and prayers.

---

[2] Roger Hazelton, *The God We Worship* (New York: The Macmillan Company, 1946), pp. 158-159.

[3] Seward Hiltner, *Pastoral Counseling* (New York: Abingdon Press, 1949), p. 223.

COORDINATE READING WITH BODILY ACTS

In the conducting of the ritual the leader has certain physical actions to perform. If these actions are not well planned, rehearsed, and executed they may impair the effectiveness of the oral interpretation. Poor execution of these physical actions may adversely affect the reader's timing and his general poise. If the reader becomes preoccupied with physical acts, he will not be thinking about the words and he will not read them well.

Moreover, his bodily action should be congruent with the meaning and mood of the ritual and appropriate to the situation in which it is executed. If the leader's bodily action is slovenly, careless, or inappropriate, it will tend to destroy the reader's personal involvement in the service and thus weaken his oral reading.

When the leader turns toward the altar, stands before it with the offering, or kneels before it to pray, he should remember that more force of voice and more vocal expressiveness are absolutely necessary. Not only is his voice projected away from the congregation, but there is no communication through facial expression.

SHOW FIRM CLEAR LEADERSHIP

The leadership of the ritual should be clear and convincing. Such directions as *Let us pray* and *Hear the words of the gospel* should be read with a strong voice, distinct enunciation, and in a firm manner. In unison prayers you should begin the prayer with a firm, clear projection of voice and a lively projection of mood, then fade out as the congregation responds and takes over the prayer. There are several reasons for emphasizing this sort of leadership in conducting the ritual. Because the worship experience of those participating in the ritual can be deeply moving, a definite and vigorous leadership is required to keep the whole congregation together through the service. Otherwise a few worshipers may linger at one point, another group may continue to ponder a different portion of the service, while the majority are trying to move along with the leader.

Particularly in the case of weddings and funerals, there may be many persons present who are not members of your congregation and, therefore, not accustomed to your leadership or familiar with some parts of the ritual which you employ. Then, too, these services will be participated in less frequently by your congregation, and they will not be as certain as to how the service will proceed as they would be of the Sunday morning worship service. Neither, with the exception of the communion service, will they have an order of worship in hand. Consequently, the only guidance they receive will be from you.

MAKE SPIRITUAL AND PHYSICAL PREPARATION FOR LEADERSHIP

In addition to a personal study of the ritual, the leader needs to quicken his spiritual appreciation for the ritual. He will want to pray for the service and for those who participate in it. He may use the scripture passages and prayers from the ritual in his own daily devotions. Moreover, he will want to read some devotional literature dealing with the ritual. When the ritual ministers to him as he reads it, he is ready to minister to others through his oral interpretation.

The act of oral interpretation requires the use of eyes, hands, bodily posture and action, voice, and mind; therefore the importance of being relaxed, rested, and generally in good health should be readily apparent. The fatigued, tense, preoccupied minister is working against tremendous odds when he turns to the oral interpretation of the ritual.

In addition to having generally good health, getting an adequate amount of sleep, and participating in relaxing activities, the minister should try to have a half-hour period prior to conducting the ritual during which he can relax, clear his mind of other concerns, and begin to focus his attention on the ritual and on those to whom he intends to minister.

In case the parish minister takes this suggestion to be a utopian dream rather than a practical necessity, let him consider this warning from Edgar N. Jackson: "One of the unfortunate facts about the professional ministry is that the preacher is so busy serving others that his own spiritual needs may be neglected. He is so busy helping others to worship that the real experience of worship may not come to him." [4]

---

[4] Edgar N. Jackson, *How to Preach to People's Needs* (New York: Abingdon Press, 1946), p. 181.

SUMMARY

Good oral interpretation makes an important contribution to the due administration of the sacraments. It is an equally significant factor in the effective conducting of weddings and funerals. However, most ministers find that they must resist several forces which tend to influence them to read in a routine and habitual manner. To overcome these influences the minister is urged to prepare himself thoroughly—studying the Biblical and theological content, the history, the structure, and the words of the ritual. He is also urged to view participation in the ritual as a shared worship experience which may become a sacred event in the lives of the participants. In addition, he is advised that a firm and clear leadership is required and that he can strengthen himself for such leadership by quickening his own spiritual appreciation of the ritual.

Chapter 17

Reading the Baptismal Ritual

Holy baptism holds first place among all the sacraments because it is the gate of spiritual life; for by it we are made members of Christ and of the body of the Church.

POPE EUGENIUS IV*

In the reading of the baptismal service, the minister should make a special effort to be aware of the uniqueness of this occasion for the persons being baptized and for the members of their families. He should also strive for this to be a "person to person" interpretation in which he really communicates to those being baptized or to their parents. In addition, he may attempt to move members of the congregation to a reaffirmation of the vows which they have taken.

Such an emphasis is necessary because it is easy to regard the ritual for baptism as a minor matter. It is a brief service, simpler than the ritual for communion, matrimony, or burial of the dead. Usually it is incorporated in the longer order of the Sunday morning worship service. The congregation does not participate in this service as directly or as fre-

* Ray C. Petry, *A History of Christianity* (Englewood Cliffs, N. J.: Prentice-Hall Inc., 1962), p. 325.

quently as it does in the communion service, nor is the congregation made up of so large a number of friends and relations as are those at the wedding and funeral services. There are fewer pressures on the pastor to give this service the preparation and presentation it deserves.

In recent years ministers have placed more emphasis on preparatory instruction for participation in baptism. It would seem that there ought to be an equal preparation by the ministers for conducting the service. A casual sight reading is hardly a fitting or satisfying conclusion to a period of instruction and preparation for participating in the ritual.

As a part of his preparation, the minister ought to refresh his mind concerning what he is saying theologically. What does this ritual say about God, about man, about the church? Is a real change effected in the recipients' spiritual state by the external rite, or is this change dependent on the faith of the recipient? Is the baptism of infants a recognition of the parents' responsibility for religious instruction? Is it something more? Every minister ought to update or refresh himself about his theological stance toward baptism each time he administers the sacrament. Vagueness and laxity about our theological understanding of the sacrament will seriously weaken our oral interpretation of the ritual.

In addition, the minister ought to review his exegesis of the Biblical passage or passages contained in the ritual for baptism. Preferably, he should prepare to read the Biblical passages in the same thorough way that he prepares to read the scripture lesson for the Sunday morning worship service. Too many ministers rely on study made some time ago and make no serious study of the passage for the present occasion. Their behavior is an offense to the Word of God and disastrous to their effort to interpret the passage orally.

Next, the minister should take specific note of the various reading tasks he must perform. He will probably find prayers, passages of Scripture, questions to be put to those to be baptized or to their parents, a declaration of the act of baptism, and a benediction. There may be an opening statement, or address, to the whole congregation. There may also be verbal rubrics such as *Let us pray* and *Hear the words of the Gospel.*

Adequate preparation for reading the ritual aloud requires an awareness of the various kinds of material, the order in which they appear, understanding of the manner of oral reading appropriate to each, and oral practices to insure that each type of material is read in an appropriate manner. One would not want the manner of reading used for the opening statement to be employed for the prayers.

THE PRAYERS

In this sacrament the prayers are of particular importance. If the prayers are not genuine and heartfelt, it is highly unlikely that this baptism will become a sacred event for those participating in it. The prayers are a particular challenge because they are prayers of intercession for those who are being baptized and, in infant baptism, for the parents as well. The only thing that will suffice is a real act of intercession.

Some ministers may protest that their difficulty lies in the reading of prepared prayers. They feel that extempore prayers would be less difficult for them and more meaningful to the people. Such ministers need to learn to read prayers so well that they can pray naturally and genuinely even though they are reading a prayer printed in the ritual. The following practices are particularly useful in this respect:

1. Become thoroughly familiar with the prayer. How does it begin? How does it end? How is it organized? What are the main items of its content? If all ministers were examined on their knowledge of the content of the prayers in the most frequently used orders of the ritual, the majority of them would be ashamed of the incompleteness and inaccuracy of their answers.
2. Ponder the prayer for its appropriateness and depth of spiritual insight. Too many worship leaders have failed to cultivate a personal appreciation of the prayers contained in the ritual.
3. Read the prayer aloud over and over again until the words come readily and easily. Indeed, the words should be so well known and easily spoken that they seem to be your own.
4. Read books on prayer which are intended to strengthen your own spiritual life prior to your oral interpretation of the ritual. Enrich your praying by considering the experience and insights of others.

> Prayer is not without the intellectual element, but it is essentially a thing of the heart. It springs from a sense of weakness and want, and from a certain spiritual aspiration. It is as certain that the heart lifts itself up to something above it as that sparks and flames lift themselves up into the air when they are kindled. The finer, the larger, the richer, the truer the natures of men are, the more a tendency toward something higher than the mere senses is shown in them. In general, the truest spirit of prayer is that which most nearly resembles the affectionate, confiding disposition of a little child.

A true praying spirit is one which holds itself in such relations to God that the mood which is predominant is constantly being opened and emptied before Him.[1]

5. Know those participating in the ceremony—those who are being baptized and parents who are bringing infants—well enough to truly pray for them. You cannot very well pray for spiritual needs about which you are uninformed. You are not likely to learn much about such needs by summoning the participants to the church and lecturing them on the meaning and obligations of baptism. You are more likely to learn about the needs of their souls by visiting their homes. Knowing of the needs of the souls before you, you must intercede fully with the Father for them. Those before you must feel that in you they have, here and now, an advocate with the Father. Are these words from *The Passion for Souls* meant for us?

> If we pray in cold blood we are no longer ministers of the Cross. True intercession is a sacrifice, a bleeding sacrifice, a perpetuation of Calvary, a "filling up" of the suffering of Christ. St. Catherine told a friend that the anguish which she experienced, in the realization of the suffering of Christ, was greatest at the moment when she was pleading for the salvation of others. "Promise me that Thou wilt save them!" she cried, and stretching forth her right hand to Jesus, she again implored in agony "Promise me, dear Lord, that Thou wilt save them. O give me a Token that Thou wilt." Then her Lord seemed to clasp her outstretched hand in His, and give her the promise, and she felt a piercing pain as though a nail had been driven through the palm. I think I know the meaning of the mystic experience. She had become so absolutely one with the interceding Saviour that she entered into the fellowship of His crucifixion. Her prayers were red with sacrifice, and she felt the grasp of the pierced hand.
>
> My brethren, this is the ministry which the Master owns. The agonized yearnings which perfect the sufferings of His own intercession. And we in the succession? Do our prayers bleed? Have we felt the painful fellowship of the pierced hand? I am so often ashamed of my prayers. They so frequently cost me nothing; they shed no blood. I am amazed at the grace and condescension of my Lord that He confers any fruitfulness upon my superficial pains.[2]

---

[1] Henry Ward Beecher, *A Book of Public Prayer* (Westwood, N. J.: Fleming H. Revell Co., 1892), pp. 11-12.

[2] J. H. Jowett, *The Passion for Souls* (Westwood, N. J.: Fleming H. Revell Co., 1905), pp. 35-36.

THE VOWS

To bring this sacrament to a climax, the vows must be read in such a manner that those who are to respond are moved to do so with their whole hearts and souls. Present the vows to them in the faith that the Holy Spirit will move them to a worthy response. In this sacrament, faith encourages faith. Let them sense your testimony that this is the Way, the Truth, and the Life, and now is the time to enter therein.

Let parents hear your testimony that you are setting before them a rich spiritual opportunity in which their cup will overflow. Let them know the joy with which you call them to fulfill these duties of Christian parents.

The minister enables the participants to respond in faith when he helps them see the vision of the new life with God, set before them in the vows. This vision of the life eternal enables your people to make the vows and to keep them. Of course, the vows cannot be read in this manner unless they have been thoroughly studied and fully appreciated. The minister should not only know what they say; he should also be aware of them as guiding and undergirding forces in his own life. They must be spiritually alive for him and rich with spiritual promise for his people.

THE CONGREGATION

To give proper leadership in the administration of this sacrament, you need the assistance of your congregation. Do not let them be mere observers. Make them spiritual participants. The opening address to the congregation must not be simply a formal announcement of what is about to take place. Rather, it needs to be an earnest appeal for spiritual participation. Seek to involve them in the prayers as you do in the pastoral prayer, so that they join you in these intercessions. If those being baptized and/or their parents sense the intercession of the whole congregation, it will be a memorable and a moving experience for them.

When the vows are given, let them be read with sufficient strength of voice, clarity of articulation, and communication of meaning that the entire congregation may empathize with those taking the vows. Those who have already taken the vows may be moved to a reaffirmation and renewal of their own vows. Those who will take such vows in the future may be moved to anticipate and reflect on the meaning and blessing of the sacrament. During the vows, too, they may be moved from the status of spectators to the experience of participants. The empathy of a congregational response will be encouraging and undergirding for the immediate participants and make them aware of the *fellowship* of believers.

THE BENEDICTION

It is important that the sacredness of the occasion—what we have understood and what we have felt—be gathered up and affirmed in the benediction. Rather than being a let-down, the benediction ought to help us lift our hearts up to God and receive His grace, mercy, and peace. If the baptism is set in the context of a worship service, particular care must be taken to avoid reciting the benediction out of habit while we mentally look ahead to see how we will re-enter the service and lead the congregation into the next act of worship.

SPECIAL PROBLEMS

In the baptismal ritual, the person or persons to be baptized may be identified as him, her, or them. Most ministers use a ritual which is printed for the baptism of one man or boy. If more than one person is being baptized or if a woman or a girl is being baptized, the minister will have to make an instantaneous change in the ritual at all the appropriate points. Usually these words are printed in italics. If the wording will have to be changed at these places, the ritual should be read aloud with these changes until they come so automatically that there are no hesitations which adversely affect either the rate or the rhythm of the reading.

Just prior to the act of baptism, the minister will want to lay the ritual aside. He should have a convenient place to lay the book where it will not be disturbed until he picks it up again for reading the remainder of the service. In addition, the page and paragraph at which he is to start should be clearly and distinctly marked.

When continuing the reading of the service, the minister should take a moment to make certain that he is ready—be sure he has found his place, caught the mood of this part of the ritual, and has an adeqaute breath supply. Then he should intensify his oral interpretation for the first sentence or two so that he takes full command of the situation and has the attention and cooperation of the whole congregation.

If the minister will adequately prepare for it, the administration of the sacrament of baptism can be a sacred event which is a joy to him and a blessing to his people.

Chapter 18

Reading the Communion Ritual

> *It is not surprising that the Last Supper has been re-enacted down the centuries. Here is a symbolic act that brings home, as no mere words can do, the great affirmations of the Christian faith. Here is a celebration that proclaims the possibility of forgiveness for sin, healing for sorrow, strength for the day, and peace within even amidst the most adverse conditions. Here for those who "draw near with faith" is the apprehension of a divine presence and power whereby the heart is cleansed, renewed, and comforted. Here is opportunity for self commitment. . . . What is essential to the spiritual value of this sacrament is the apprehension of the presence of Christ, personal response to the call of God revealed in him, and hearty participation in the fellowship which he brought into being. . . . Spiritual communion with Christ involves that we will share his love to God and men.*
>
> E. F. Tittle*

One of the most humbling and inspiring tasks which the minister undertakes is the administration of holy communion. It is both a high privilege and a heavy responsibility. It was initiated by our Lord, and it is He who has commanded us to continue it. Moreover, this sacrament has a deep and saving meaning for the communicants. They truly feed

---

* *The Gospel According to Luke* (New York: Harper & Row, Publishers, 1951), pp. 234-235.

on Him in their hearts by faith, and they leave the service in thanksgiving.

These compelling reasons for reading the service aloud in the best manner possible are countered by the difficult nature of the content of the ritual as well as the complexities of administering this particular sacrament. Rigorous, thorough preparation and review are necessary for reading the ritual aloud effectively.

It should be emphasized at the outset that oral interpretation of the ritual cannot be separated from the general administration of the sacrament. They are related in meaning, for the meaning of this sacrament is communicated through both word and deed.

Moreover, the skill with which they are used has a reciprocal effect. Good oral interpretation prompts alert, dignified, communicative bodily action. Well-executed, appropriate, meaningful bodily action stimulates appropriate and meaningful oral interpretation of the ritual. Likewise, casual and slovenly bodily action leads to similar characteristics in the oral reading of the ritual. Mary Virginia Fredricks stressed the importance of this interdependence of speech and bodily action in her doctoral dissertation:

> The student who comes to the speech situation, particularly to the oral interpretation situation, must be made aware that he brings with him his total physical being that not only can but must be involved in the speech act. Speech is action. It is gesture. The individual's total biological organism is a legitimate and essential part of the speech act.[1]

In addition, these two parts of the leader's effort are linked together in the worship experience of the congregation. Once after a communion service, a fellow worshiper complained to me that he had been so disturbed by the way the minister knelt at the altar that he could not join in the prayer of consecration. "He looked like he was going to shoot craps," observed the disgruntled worshiper. To put it bluntly, if we want our oral interpretation of the ritual to be rightly heard, we had better take pains to look like we are leading a worship service and not like we are doing something else. Although this chapter will not offer advice on the proper use of bodily action for the leadership of the com-

[1] Mary Virginia Fredricks, "An Approach to the Teaching of Oral Interpretation in Terms of Dramatic Action" (Doctoral Dissertation, University of Minnesota, 1961), p. 3.

munion service, keep in mind the close correlation between the words of leadership and acts of leadership, and remember that effective oral interpretation requires able and appropriate use of the body in the acts of leadership.

Another factor which directly affects the oral interpretation of the communion ritual is time. Far too many ministers habitually carry the communion service beyond the normal time for dismissal. They are conscious throughout the communion service of the need to move along. As a result they read more rapidly than is natural for them. Consequently their communicativeness is seriously inhibited, as it is impossible to hurry and communicate the full meaning of the ritual at the same time. In deed as well as word the leader may communicate impatience and anxiety instead of God's love. If the leader wants to read the communion ritual well, the complete service should be carefully timed and prepared so that it will dismiss three to five minutes before the appointed time. Only when the minister knows that the service has been timed (and can be completed a few minutes before the regular time for dismissal) will he be able to relax and read at a rate that will be natural. Thus he will fully communicate the profound meaning of the sacrament.

FAMILIARITY WITH THE ORDER

Every reader should be aware of the various parts of the communion ritual and the significance of each part. There is, of course, considerable variation among different denominations. Even within the same denomination, there may be alternate orders for the observance of the sacrament. However, the following items are widely used as a complete service or as parts of a longer order for the celebration of holy communion.

Usually there is a scripture lesson. In longer orders both the Ten Commandments and the Beatitudes may be read. As an alternative to the reading of the Ten Commandments, the first part of the 53rd chapter of Isaiah is sometimes read responsively. If the scripture passage is selected by the minister, it may be a passage from the Gospels describing the institution of the sacrament or a passage from the Epistles dealing with the due observance of the sacrament.

At the very least, the reading of the Scriptures ought to be an able reading resulting from the thorough study and preparation described in

Chapter 13. In addition, the scripture reading ought to be permeated with a vivid sense of the relevance of this passage for the people participating in this particular celebration of the sacrament. If we are reading the commandment to remember the Sabbath day and keep it holy, let us pray for those before us who are in torment of soul because they fail to adequately observe a Sabbath and thus have no satisfying communion with God.

When prayer is offered, the leader ought to pour out his own soul for the sake of those communicants who are unresponsive. Prayer is the pathway to the Lord's table. In every moment of his leadership, the minister's earnest pastoral invitation (*Pray with me*) ought to be felt keenly by each worshiper. Moreover, these prayers should be uttered from the depths of our souls. In them, parishioners should sense the profound meaning.

The Reverend Peter Green, once Canon of Manchester, also affirms the importance of prayer in the communion service:

> The Eucharist is the Church's prayer meeting, and Jesus is the great Intercessor. He intercedes for us, and He offers our prayers to God the Father; for all our prayers are offered "through Jesus Christ our Lord." There is no time, and no place, for prayer better than the Eucharist.[2]

When the time arrives to invite the congregation to participate in the sacrament, the invitation should be read in awe and faith—awe of God's grace and faith that men reverently await the invitation. Thomas à Kempis lifts up the awesomeness of the moment for us:

> O sweet and loving word in the ear of a sinner, that Thou, my Lord God, shouldst invite the poor and needy to the participation of Thy most holy body!
>
> But who am I, Lord, that I should presume to approach unto Thee?
>
> Behold, the heaven of heavens can not contain Thee, and Thou sayest, "Come ye all unto me."
>
> What meaneth this so gracious a condescension and this so loving invitation?
>
> How shall I dare to come, who know not any good in myself, whereupon I may presume?
>
> How shall I bring Thee into my house, I that have so often offended Thy most benign countenance?

[2] Peter Green, *This Holy Fellowship* (New York: Longmans, Green & Co., Inc., 1935), p. 97.

> Angels and archangels stand in awe of Thee; saints and righteous men do fear Thee, and sayest Thou "Come ye all unto me?"
>
> Unless Thou, O Lord didst say this, who would believe it to be true?
>
> And unless Thou didst command it, who could attempt to draw near unto Thee? [3]

The invitation should be read in the faith that God truly wishes those present to come forward and commune. Also it should be read in the faith that those who are assembled genuinely desire to be partakers of the divine nature. If the minister does not read the invitation in such a manner, the parishioners may feel that he is presenting a false invitation. Surely we can present the invitation in the faith that this sacrifice was indeed sufficient for the sins of the whole world and that the better man in each of us yearns to respond to so gracious an invitation.

Along with awe and faith, the invitation must also be extended with love—Christian love for each soul present. Members of the congregation should be made to feel that in the issuing of the invitation the love of God is spread abroad in their hearts. By extending the invitation with Christian love, the minister may quicken its worthy reception.

Shortly before the distribution of the elements, the minister will offer the Prayer of Consecration or the Eucharistic Prayer or say the Words of Institution. At this point, when we give thanks and adore God, the congregation should be lead into a state of awe and deep gratitude for the wondrous love of God made known to us in the institution of the Lord's Supper.

In order to offer the prayer or say the Words of Institution in the awesome wonder and joy they merit, the leader must imaginatively participate in that institution—he must hear not only *what* was said but *how* it was said. He must see what was done and sense the manner and mood in which it was done. As Dr. Curry remarks:

> The function of imagination in expression is a very important one. . . . We hear it continually said by students, "Oh, if I could only speak some of my own thoughts, or if I could talk about a scene that I saw, I could feel it," but this is a mistake, for the lack of imagination is as apparent in speech as in recitation. No man living ever saw the cross upon which Christ was crucified or knows the real Calvary. Even if the real spot were known, two thousand years have changed the very stones upon which stepped those feet which "were nailed for

---

[3] Thomas à Kempis, *Imitation of Christ* (New York: Hurst & Co., 1843), p. 253.

> our advantage on a bitter cross." What is left must be ideal, even as we stand under the few relics of trees which are called by tradition Gethsemane. To see Gethsemane requires imagination. The Sea of Galilee, without imagination, would lack all power to awaken feeling. As a mere sheet of water it would not compare with Lucerne, if feeling must arise from what is seen. . . . The highest requisite of a good speaker, a good reader, is to see what is not visible to the eyes, to realize in imagination every situation, to see the end from the beginning by the imagination, and to realize a unity of purpose in each successive idea.[4]

To interpret the prayer or the words of institution, the minister must imagine himself in the Upper Room and become a participant in that first Lord's Supper. He must behold the wondrous love of Jesus, who could still look with compassion on those disciples when they did not comprehend His kingdom, were blind to His betrayal, and were apathetic toward His agony.

Taking all that remained to Him—a little time and the passover meal which they had planned to eat together—He sought in simple words and deeds to write the meaning of the cross so indelibly on their hearts that none of the coming events would be able to erase it. Then came the most inspired moment of teaching in all human history. The disciples saw the broken bread, handled it, smelled it, tasted it, and heard the words, "This is My body which is broken for you." How carefully, deliberately, and earnestly must Jesus have spoken these words! How intently He must have looked into the face of each disciple, seeking assurance that they had heard and understood! After they had partaken of the cup in a like manner, Jesus gave them a directive—"As oft as ye do this, do it in remembrance of Me." How Jesus loved them—how He loved us! So patiently, so gently, so painstakingly did He prepare us—faithless, unbelieving sinners—for His crucifixion.

In some such manner the minister must imaginatively enter the Upper Room with the disciples and behold divine love preparing mankind for the crucifixion of the Saviour. Then he will be ready to offer the Eucharistic Prayer or to read the Words of Institution.

If the communicants come forward to the chancel or communion rail and kneel there to receive the elements, the words of dismissal must be firm, clear, and definite when they are dismissed, with emphasis on such words as *Rise and go*. If the words of dismissal are inaudible or indefinite,

---

[4] S. S. Curry, *The Province of Expression* (Boston, School of Expression, 1891), pp. 89-90.

confusion and embarrassment may interrupt the worship of the communicants.

PERSONAL PREPARATION

Few ministers can conduct a worshipful communion service without feeding their minds and souls prior to administration of the sacrament. They may read devotional books based on the communion ritual—such works as *Not by Bread Alone, This Holy Fellowship,* and Section Four of *Imitation of Christ.* Each day of the week preceding the communion service they may use some part of the communion ritual as a guide for their own meditation and devotions. Reading of religious verse inspired by the sacrament may also prompt a deeper contemplation of the meaning of holy communion.

THE CHERISHED CHALICE

the cherished chalice
glows polished
upon the Table
as a magnet
making parched dry
mouths to water,

to water to dryness
for the long ago drained
last drop—

The Vinedresser
has been barred
from the vineyard
and there is no turning
water into wine. . . .

There is only chalice polishing.

Marilyn Plowman

BORN OUT OF DARKNESS

We are born out of darkness
into darkness
of caves

and whales' bellies
and tunnels
and subways
and bomb shelters
and tombs.

The gravecloth is raised
from the Passover spread
And we partake of the Body
which is no longer there.

And we are born by the light
which shows who we are
over and against the darkness
in the expanse of earth and sky
and being and doing
and seeing and feeling
and living eternally.

Marilyn Plowman

As indicated earlier in this chapter, the minister ought to reaffirm or review his theological position in regard to the sacrament. How does he view transubstantiation, consubstantiation, or the receiving of the Real Presence? Reflecting on the theories of atonement which inform his position will be equally beneficial. Is Christ on the cross a ransom or a sacrifice? Does he save us *from* God or *to* God?

Words like the following from Ferre's *The Christian Fellowship* may help us to begin some serious thinking and lift the fog that beclouds the mind of many a minister who attempts to administer this sacrament effectively:

> . . . the sacraments are a means of grace in virtue of that symbolic principle of historic existence through which the significant rites of any fellowship are actually the means of its continuity and of the promotion of its purposes. In a most effectual sense God's grace is conveyed by means of sacramental symbolism. . . .
>
> If spiritual life here depends on the eating of physical food, if the spirit in this life is dependent upon the body, why cannot bread and wine offered by the church in Christ's name constitute spiritual food effective of spiritual grace? [5]

[5] Nels F. S. Ferre, *The Christian Fellowship* (New York: Harper & Row, Publishers, 1940), pp. 155, 159.

The point of this emphasis on personal preparation is that no minister can duly interpret this sacrament to others unless he has first fed on Him in his own heart with faith and thanksgiving.

SUMMARY

In this chapter you have been urged to plan the communion service carefully, giving thought to your movement about the chancel and to the timing of the service. You have also been advised to analyze the service, giving individual attention to such parts as the scripture lesson, prayers, invitation, and the Words of Institution (Prayer of Consecration). In addition, you have been admonished to personally prepare yourself both mentally and spiritually for orally interpreting the ritual. Keep before you the meaning which this service can have for your parishioners, if it is duly administered. Let all that we do and say in conducting and orally interpreting the holy communion service suggest to the congregation such thoughts as those voiced by John Wesley in his sermon "The Means of Grace":

> Is not the eating of that bread and the drinking of that cup the outward and visible means whereby God conveys into our souls all that spiritual grace, that righteousness and peace, that joy in the Holy Ghost, which were purchased by the body of Christ once broken, and the blood of Christ once shed for us? Let us all, therefore, who truly desire the grace of God, eat of that bread and drink of that cup.[6]

[6] *The Standard Sermons of John Wesley*, annotated by E. H. Sugden (London: The Epworth Press, 1935), p. 253.

Chapter 19

Reading the Wedding Ritual

Let those "Whom God has joined together" come to see through the eyes of God and they will not make mountains out of molehills. Let them come to know from personal experience that God is able in any situation to uphold those who trust Him, and they will not be frightened of the necessity for economy or any other demand that life is making upon them. They will have the confidence that God is with them and will see them through. "Those whom God has joined together" have a good hope of making their marriage a success if at the start they dedicate themselves to God and His purpose of good in the world.

E. F. TITTLE*

Our goal in reading the marriage ritual should be to help the couple before us dedicate themselves to God and His purpose of good in the world. Along with this aim, we can also hope to help those contemplating marriage to sense the importance of such a dedication as well as to assist those married couples in the congregation to renew their dedication to God.

If you hope to help the couple rise above the experiences of preparing for the service, the consciousness of being the focus of the congregation's attention, and their uncertainty about the future, you yourself must turn to God and fix your attention fully on Him. Only if you are

* "What God Has Joined Together," *The First Church Pulpit,* VI, No. 12 (Evanston, Illinois: The First Methodist Church, 1943), pp. 11-12.

keenly aware of God joining these two persons together will they have any awareness of it. When you read, "We are gathered in the sight of God and the presence of these witnesses," you need to believe and feel that this is really so—that God is here. As Seward Hiltner observes:

> The service of marriage is old, but the various symbols connected with it suggest on a level deeper than consciousness both the indissoluble character of the union—seen in the circular ring—and the social character of marriage—"God and this company." [1]

It is also important that you be thoroughly familiar with each part of the service, and that you move readily and surely from one unit to another. The ascent of the service to the level of the sacred should not be broken by inept handling of the transitions from one section to another. Pause before each new section. Set the mood appropriate for it in your own thinking and feeling. Get a firm grasp of the opening words of the next unit, then start to read the new section. Do not let the situation, nor the persons present, panic you into starting the new unit before you have caught the mood and have the opening words clearly in mind.

OPENING THE SERVICE

In the opening words of the ritual, the minister affirms that this ceremony is more than a witnessing by public act to the social nature of the marriage contract. This is a time of worship, for marriage is a holy estate.

This opening announcement requires firmness and strength of voice, for it is directed to the whole congregation. As the minister reads this first unit, he should look at the wedding party and at the congregation as well. Through interpretation of meaning, projection of voice, and eye contact, he should read the ritual to the entire congregation. The following paragraph, taken from a ritual of worship for marriage, states the mood of corporate worship which should be created through the interpretation of this first unit of the service:

> As the ceremony proceeds, members of the congregation are encouraged to be in the spirit and attitude of worship. No married

[1] Seward Hiltner, *Pastoral Counseling* (New York: Abingdon Press, 1949), pp. 223-24.

person present should miss the opportunity of giving thanks to God for his own marriage, and of silently renewing his own vows that are now being taken for the first time by others. No guest should leave the service without praying that God's many blessings may truly rest upon this man and this woman all the days of their life together.[2]

QUESTIONS

The manner in which the questions are put to the couple is important. They ought not to be asked in a weak or apologetic manner. Neither ought they be put in the style of a cross-examination. The questions should be presented as an opportunity to publicly profess their love and to declare in God's presence their willingness to assume the responsibilities of Christian marriage.

The question "Who giveth this woman . . ." should be voiced for the whole congregation to hear, and voiced in a cordial manner. This is a question asking for information and it can be concluded with a rising vocal inflection.

These questions ought not to be read in a mechanical way. Let the reader be suspicious of an automatic grouping. Let him also avoid any tendency to keep the voice at a constant lower pitch level. The questions should be specifically interpreted for this particular ceremony. It may be that one of the conditions or requirements will be especially significant for this couple.

VOWS

In the vows, the participants repeat the words after the minister, and he has the opportunity to lead the marriage partners into an expression of love and loyalty which they may not have been able to voice prior to this occasion. Do not always group and pace these vows in exactly the same way. Group and pace the vows in accordance with the ability of each respondent. Avoid formality and stiffness of vocal manner. Strive for full vocal responsiveness and expression of feeling. If the vow moves naturally to a climax, sense it and lead the respondent into it. The participation of the couple in this part of the service will be strongly affected by your interpretation of these vows.

---

[2] Allan R. Ressor, "A Wedding Can Be an Act of Worship," *Christian Advocate,* VII, No. 13 (1963), p. 16.

When the ring (or rings) is given, do not be too anxious to initiate the vow which accompanies this act. Allow the participant ample time to place the ring and to give you his attention. It is proper to advise the bride and groom that the ring may be started on the finger and the wearer may move it down over the larger knuckle at a later time. This will allow the service to proceed without undue delay or personal embarrassment.

PRAYERS

The prayers, too, are vital to the service and its meaning for the participants. The minister should take time to pray deeply. The full meaning of the words should be sounded. Moreover, the prayer should be prayed for this particular couple. If the minister begins to pray for this couple in his own daily prayers soon after he has agreed to marry them, he will find it easier to personalize the prayer in the ritual. Some ministers insert the first names of the man and woman being married at the appropriate places in the prayer. Instead of saying, "this man and this woman," they would say, "John and Mary."

The minister should earnestly strive to involve the couple in these prayers. Even though they are intercessary prayers for the couple, they will be deeply grateful if the minister can so pastor them through his leadership that they are enabled to pray, too. When we ourselves are moved to pray, then it is that the event becomes sacred for us. The congregation, too, should feel that they are expected to join you in praying for this couple. Some ministers alter the traditional directive *Let us pray* and read it instead as *Let us all pray*. They do this in order to stress that the entire congregation is being called to prayer. If such is their experience during the service, the members of the wedding party and the congregation will be more ready to genuinely pray the Lord's Prayer at the close of the service.

CONCLUDING THE SERVICE

The declaration or pronouncement of marriage should be strong, clear, and joyous. Surely it ought not to be done with waning vocal projection or slovenly articulation. It should be directed to the congregation with both voice and eye contact.

Great care should be taken to insure that you will use the right names and that you will pronounce them accurately. At a wedding I attended, the bride's sister was the maid of honor, and the minister spoke the sister's name rather than the bride's name. Although such an error can be easily understood, nonetheless it is so distracting to those participating in the service that every precaution should be taken to avoid it. As mentioned in an earlier chapter, copies of the wedding ritual which have blank spaces where the minister may write in the names of the bride and groom are available at nominal cost. This is one way of avoiding such a mistake.

The benediction should be in accord with the mood of the service, and it should be fully interpreted. The service should not just fade away as the minister pronounces it. The rituals of several denominations instruct the minister to pronounce the benediction as a blessing on the couple who have been united in marriage. This calls for a different tone and manner than the dismissal of the Sunday morning congregation. The minister ought to take care not to fall into his habitual pattern of pronouncing the benediction.

LEADERSHIP

The minister should coördinate the participation of all present through strong, effective leadership. He should be certain of his role and fulfill it well. Enter into the service rather than remaining withdrawn from it. Initiate each unit firmly and distinctly. Look to those who are to participate with expectation as a director of a choir or orchestra might look to various musicians for their response. Evidence in voice and bodily action the meaning which you find in the ritual and your appreciation for the beauty and dignity of the service. Mary Virginia Fredricks emphasizes the importance of outward manifestation of your response to the ritual: ". . . it is not enough that the reader respond privately or inwardly. Unless he manifests his response through accurate and active visible and vocal symbols, he cannot evoke an active response to the literature on the part of the audience." [3] In this service, as in baptism and communion, spiritual leadership is of prime importance.

If the minister assumes a firm leadership role, the other participants

[3] Mary Virginia Fredricks, "An Approach to the Teaching of Oral Interpretation in Terms of Dramatic Action" (Doctoral Dissertation, University of Minnesota, 1961), p. 18.

can relax and concentrate fully on their own roles with the knowledge that if they are in any doubt as to how to proceed they can turn to him for guidance. It is well to make this matter explicit and clear during the wedding rehearsal. Such instruction and assurance will make a constructive contribution to the participation of all those in the wedding party.

Let the minister's attitude during the rehearsal and during the ceremony itself be influenced by such observations as these words of Tertullian:

> Whence do we find adequate words to tell fully of the happiness of that marriage which the church cements and the oblation confirms, and the benediction seals; which the angels announce, and the Father holds for ratified. . . . What kind of yoke is that of two believers of one hope, one discipline, and the same service? The two are brethren, two are fellow servants, no difference of spirit or flesh; nay, truly, two in one flesh; where there is one flesh, the spirit is one.[4]

[4] Ray C. Petry, *A History of Christianity* (Englewood Cliffs, N. J.: Prentice-Hall, Inc., 1962), pp. 98-99.

Chapter 20

Reading the Funeral Ritual

> *It is the Christian's rightful faith that, however dark the night, God's love surrounds us. Whether we find Him near or far, or cry out in anguish but hear no answering word, we can still know that God has not forsaken us. When we are assured that God ceases not to love us, we can watch in patience through the night and wait for the dawn. Then as God finds us and speaks to our waiting spirits, peace and power flow into our lives.*
>
> GEORGIA HARKNESS*

The funeral is an occasion when we are all aware of our need for a strength which is more than our own. Ministering to those immediately bereaved, to those still grieving for loved ones long departed, to those anticipating their own death or the death of a loved one, and to others as well, the funeral ritual demands a thorough knowledge and command of the materials to be read, a full sharing of their content in voice, eye contact, and mood, and an appreciative sensitivity for the occasion. The oral interpretation of the funeral ritual should be fully appropriate and adequate in all respects.

As in the case of the wedding, the funeral should be a *worship* service.

> The Christian funeral is a service of worship, a service of praise and thanksgiving for the life in which we have shared, for the gift of

* *The Dark Night of the Soul* (New York: Abingdon Press, 1945), p. 170.

> fellowship with God after death has ended this life, and for the abiding presence of the Holy Spirit, who holds us up in time of need. All attending the funeral join in worship as a response to God's love, and in doing so support those who grieve.
>
> The funeral is not a service performed by the pastor. It is congregational worship in which the congregation shares the comfort, strength, and encouragement of faith with those who grieve.[1]

The preceding observations provide us with some practical suggestions for the oral interpretation of the funeral ritual.

1. The reader ought to be clear about his own beliefs concerning man, God, death, resurrection, and eternal life. Fuzziness in his own thinking on these subjects will *not* assist him to interpret the funeral ritual more effectively.
2. The aim of the interpretation is to evoke worship—worship by the entire congregation. Together we draw near to God from whom our help comes.
3. The reading is directed to the entire congregation. The ministry of the funeral service is an inclusive ministry. As suggested in the opening paragraph of this chapter, most of your funeral congregation will have some experience with death and will be looking for help. This means that vocal projection, projection of mood or feeling, bodily action, and eye contact must be adequate for communication to the entire congregation and not just to the members of the immediate family.

RATE OF READING

In Chapter 9, "The Use of Time in Oral Reading," the reader was advised to consider three things in determining his rate of reading—the content of the selection, the ability of the audience to receive and respond, and the ability of the reader. Normally, all three of these factors will suggest an unhurried, even deliberate reading for the funeral service. The Scriptures, the prayers, the hymns or poems, and the words of the funeral meditation will all deal with deep, profound ideas, and will not be well expressed by a rapid or even a casual rate of reading.

Members of the congregation who are moved by this death (or by an earlier bereavement brought vividly to mind by this occasion) will not

[1] Edwin B. Womack, "I Stopped Conducting Pagan Funerals," *Christian Advocate,* VII, No. 14 (1963), pp. 12-13.

be in the mood to race along after the reader. Members of the immediate family may be fatigued, grief-stricken, even shocked. They may well be incapable of rapid listening and response.

From the standpoint of your own communicative effort, you will probably be able to have more control and suggest more of the deeper meaning of what you read *if* you read in an unhurried, deliberate manner.

Because all three criteria indicate a slower pace, the use of the pause is as vital to the reading of the funeral service as it is to any other part of the ritual. Dr. Curry's advice about the use of pauses is pertinent at this point:

> Pause is the first remedy for the monotonous and meaningless calling of words so common in the reading of the Scriptures. A false reverence for the mere words sometimes apparently prevents the reader from identifying himself genuinely with the thought and the situation.[2]

We particularly desire to avoid a monotonous and meaningless calling of words when reading the funeral service; therefore, we should plan and practice the use of pauses for the oral interpretation of the service. In addition, we should strive to develop our ability to make good judgments regarding the desirable duration of pauses, both in terms of the content and in terms of how it is being heard.

THE SCRIPTURES

Not only should the Scriptures be read at a deliberate rate, with care given to the use of pauses, but they should be read with deep appreciation for their meaning. This appreciation should spring from the same sort of careful preparation and study recommended in Chapter 13 for the reading of the scripture lesson in the formal worship service on Sunday morning. As soon as the funeral arrangements have been made, the minister should select his scripture passages and begin to study and prepare them. The way he read them at the previous funeral will not do. He should prepare afresh for each funeral. If he does not, recall and habit will soon crowd out interpretation.

Moreover, this study must not be just a quick review of the historical-critical analysis of the passage. Your study and preparation of the scrip-

[2] S. S. Curry, *Vocal and Literary Interpretation of the Bible* (New York: The Macmillan Company, 1903), p. 145.

ture passage should lead to appreciation through understanding of the religious insights and of the way in which they are expressed.

Frequently the minister reads several passages of Scripture in succession. Between these selections he should pause and refresh his mind as to the meaning and mood of the next passage. Then, as the meaning and mood of the passage begin to speak to him, he should start to read it aloud. Too many ministers read right on from one selection to another as though all selections were all of the same mood and meant the same thing.

THE PRAYERS

A goodly number of the people who come to funerals expect to do some serious praying. In reading these prayers, the minister should sound the breadth and depth of their meaning. Every word ought to carry its weight. A layman in the first church I served taught me how much can be put into a single word at the time of bereavement. He would stand before the persons he was seeking to console, take their hands in his, look them in the eye for several seconds, then say very slowly and deliberately "Sympathy," look into their eyes for a few seconds longer, loose their hands and go on. Usually he would say more to the bereaved person with this one word than anyone else who might speak.

In addition to reading the prayers deliberately and giving full value to individual words, we will also need a relaxed and responsive vocal mechanism to express the fine shades and depths of meaning. If the minister is moved by the grief of the mourners, he may discover a feeling of tenseness and strain in his throat. The suggestions given in Chapter 6 for relaxing the throat should be utilized. Regular, deep breathing, with the use of swallowing and inaudible sighs to keep the throat open and relaxed, should be of aid to the reader.

As these prayers are intercessory in character, the minister should use a voice and manner adequate to represent the intercession of the whole congregation for those who grieve, and there should be sufficient variety in vocal quality to suggest that this is specific intercession for individuals known to you and for whom you covet God's loving care.

If several prayers are read together, as in the case of the Biblical selections, the reader should pause between each one—getting the mood and content of the next prayer in mind, and then reading the prayer aloud. The interpretation of all the prayers should not be limited to one mood and one manner of reading. Again, as in the case of the Biblical passages, the prayers should be selected early and carefully studied and prepared for this funeral. Do not rely on previous use of the prayers as adequate preparation for this occasion.

THE MOOD

Nothing less than total concentration on the task of reading the funeral ritual aloud will do. The depth of meaning and mood which you desire to interpret demands it. The nature of the occasion demands it. In addition, because this service is of the utmost concern to the bereaved, it must also be of the same concern to you. Any preoccupation with other ministerial tasks or with other parts of the funeral service is likely to be taken as an offense, raising a barrier between you and those to whom you are interpreting the ritual. The mental set of your congregation demands your complete concentration on the content of the ritual and its interpretation.

THE BENEDICTION

In the interpretation of the benediction the minister should match the fullness of its meaning to the felt need of the congregation. Read deliberately, giving a full measure of emphasis to the key words.

THE COMMITTAL

At the grave, let your leadership be firm, deliberate, and definite. The difficulty of this time for the bereaved as well as the nature of the cemetery situation calls for ample projection of voice, full sharing of mood, strong execution of emphasis, and eye contact with the congregation during the reading of the scripture sentences and the words of committal.

The minister should maintain a certain reserve of energy to be used for the committal service, because stronger vocal projection, fuller communication of meaning and mood, and firmer leadership are needed at the time of committal. Moreover, the minister should avoid the mental attitude that the main task has been finished when the service in the church or funeral home has been completed. The committal should be viewed as a continuation or even as the climax of this service. At the grave, too, we should be worshiping God. The needs of those immediately bereaved and the characteristics of the outdoor setting require firmness and abandon in leadership. Remember that many of the people attending the committal will have attended a committal less frequently than a service in a church or mortuary and, consequently, will be less familiar with its form and with what may be expected of them.

At the time of committal as well as during the reading of the ritual for the funeral service the minister may be further assisted by Seward Hiltner's description of the pastor's role as that of "standing by" and "supportive." He also stresses that "Playing well a supportive role may lead to counseling when it is needed." [3]

If the minister does make use of hymns or poems in addition to (or in place of) portions of the ritual, these should be selected early and prepared carefully in accordance with the suggestions given in Chapter 11.

Finally, the scripture selections, prayers, and other literature to be used should be clearly designated and accurately arranged so that the mood and pace of the service are not disrupted by uncertainty as to which selections are to be read or in what order. As remarked earlier, the ritual or prayer book from which you plan to read should be equally serviceable in the sanctuary and at the grave.

As the minister comes to interpret the funeral ritual, let him bring a character and spirit similar to that attributed to Phillips Brooks by Dean Brown:

> He was a man of God, a lover of his fellows, a benign and sympathetic spirit, reaching out the hand of help to each one of us that he might lift us up. . . . It was deep calling unto deep, bringing up from profounder sources of motive and stimulus those new impulses which sent us out to run the race set before us with a finer and firmer purpose.[4]

---

[3] Seward Hiltner, *Pastoral Counseling* (New York: Abingdon Press, 1946), pp. 136-37.

[4] Charles Reynolds Brown, *The Art of Preaching* (New York: The Macmillan Company, 1922), p. 176.

Index